DEER PROOFING
your yard & garden

RHONDA MASSINGHAM HART

A *Storey Publishing Book*

STOREY
Storey Communications, Inc.
Schoolhouse Road
Pownal, Vermont 05261

The mission of Storey Communications is to serve our customers by publishing practical information that encourages personal independence in harmony with the environment.

Edited by Gwen Steege and William Overstreet
Cover and text design by Mark Tomasi
Cover photograph/illustration by Crandall & Crandall
Text production by Potter Publishing Studio
Line drawings by Becky Turner
Indexed by Barbara Hagerty

    The information in this book is true and complete to the best of our knowledge. All recommendations are made without guarantee on the part of the author or Storey Communications, Inc. The author and publisher disclaim any liability in connection with the use of this information. For additional information please contact Storey Communications, Inc., Schoolhouse Road, Pownal, Vermont 05261.

    Storey Publishing books are available for special premium and promotional uses and for customized editions. For further information, please call the Custom Publishing Department at 800-793-9396.

Printed in the United States by Vicks Lithograph & Printing Corporation
10 9 8 7 6 5 4 3 2 1

Library of Congress Cataloging-in-Publication Data

Hart, Rhonda Massingham, 1959–
     Deer-proofing your yard & garden / by Rhonda Massingham Hart.
         p.   cm.
     "A Storey Publishing book."
     ISBN 0-88266-988-5 (alk. paper)
      1. Deer—Control. 2. Wildlife depredation.   I. Title.
SB994.D4H375
635'.0496965—dc20   97-17288
                                                                      CIP

CONT [barcode] D0361042

DEDICATION

. . . for Trumpkinland

and all who belong there.
Especially my wonderful,
whimsical,
practical,
loving, giving,
hardworking,
fascinating friend,
Fran Ogren.

ACKNOWLEDGMENTS

I would like to thank the dozens of gardeners who shared their stories, frustrations, and insights into gardening in "deer country." There are truly many perspectives on the issue of deer damage control.

Also, my deepest thanks to Gwen Steege, Bill Overstreet, Elaine Sanborn, and the other great folks at Storey for their encouragement and help.

And always, my gratitude and constant thanks in all things go to Jesus Christ. With God all things are possible. Even for me.

Where Deer Are Found

Deer inhabit almost every niche of the North American continent. Among nature's most adaptable creatures, they can be found in all forty-eight contiguous states and eight Canadian provinces. Even areas without deer sometimes support their relatives: elk, moose, and caribou. Deer make themselves at home along windblown coastlines, throughout inland hills and valleys, upon majestic mountains, on high plains, and in sparse deserts. They thrive in bogs and swamps or in arid conditions. They can survive almost anywhere. And there seem to be more of them all the time.

DEER POPULATION IN PAST, PRESENT, AND FUTURE

Because deer are so plentiful now, it's easy to assume they always were and always will be. But history has a way of contradicting our assumptions about both past and future. As the role of deer in human culture changed, so did the impact of humans on the very existence of deer.

Once upon a Time

For centuries many Native Americans depended upon deer as much as we now depend upon supermarkets. Those living in or near wooded areas, particularly in the East, relied upon the plentiful deer for many of the essentials: food (venison), fashion (buckskin and pelts), and function (bones, antlers, and sinew for tools and sewing). Because of this importance, the deer became a sacred image for many tribes.

Early American settlers quickly learned the value of deer. Imagine their delight, upon landing in the bountiful wilderness of the New World, at the abundant wildlife at their disposal. They trapped beavers and muskrats for hides; hunted wild turkeys, pheasants, and grouse for supper; snared squirrels and rabbits for both meat and pelts. But none could rival deer in importance. The well-documented journals of the Lewis and Clark expedition from St. Louis, Missouri, through the Dakotas and west to the Pacific Ocean are replete with such entries as "18th of April Thursday 1805 . . . the game such as Buffalow Elk, antelopes & Deer verry plenty."

The newcomers proved to be more aggressive hunters than their predecessors. Deer provided all the same necessities for the settlers as for the native peoples, but deer also supplied major trade commodities for the relentless appetites of Europe. Soon settlers outnumbered the Natives, and the demand for venison and deerskin skyrocketed. In addition, by the mid-1700s professional hunters flooded the woods. Records of the

"I ascended to the top of the cutt bluff this morning, from whence I had a most delight-full view of the country, the whole of which except the vally formed by the Missouri is void of timber or under-brush, exposing to the first glance of the spectator immense herds of Buffaloe, Elk, deer, & Antelopes feeding in one common and bound-less pasture . . ."

Meriwether Lewis, *The Journals of the Lewis & Clark Expedition,* 1804–1806 day reflect that individual hunters often took over fifty deer in a single season, or twenty-five hundred or more throughout a career. And there were many of these hunters. From 1755 to 1773, traders shipped hides from six hundred thousand white-tailed deer from the port of Savannah, Georgia, alone. In those days, it would seem many people regarded all natural resources, including deer, as infinite.

> "One man still preserves the horns of the last deer that was killed in this vicinity, and another has told me of the particulars of the hunt in which his uncle was engaged. The hunters were formerly a numerous and merry crew here."
>
> Henry David Thoreau,
> *Walden,* 1854

Working backwards, wildlife experts gauge that before Europeans arrived on the scene North America may have supported roughly fifty-three million deer, forty million of them whitetails. By the turn of the twentieth century, fewer than five hundred thousand whitetails remained, with a count of under two hundred in the state of New Jersey. Not only were deer not an infinite resource, but they also were in real danger of disappearing forever.

So why are there so many deer today?

The Here and Now

Eventually, public awareness, being the powerful political force that it is, compelled laws, and strict adherence to those laws, to protect the dwindling deer populations. Once legislators curtailed unlimited hunting, deer populations began to rebound. In an effort to assist nature, some states, including New Jersey, resorted to importing deer. Mule deer and black-tailed deer in the West still had to contend with competition for food and habitat from domestic sheep, which notoriously overgraze land. But adaptability persevered, and the deer have made an impressive comeback across the continent.

Deer populations are tricky to estimate and track unless researchers select a given area for a full-blown physical study of habitats and inhabitants, complete with capture and tagging. Nevertheless, experts calculate that deer populations

White-tailed deer

Mule deer

White-tailed deer
and Mule deer

Distribution of deer species

throughout the United States have tripled since 1980, leading many people to speculate that more deer inhabit North America than ever! Compilations from state game departments estimate between twenty-four and thirty million whitetails and roughly five million mule deer and blacktails. Even the Columbia whitetail, once nearly extinct, has recovered to the point where it may be taken off the endangered species list.

As the distribution map above illustrates, one or more species of native deer — whitetails, mule deer, and blacktails — inhabit virtually every microenvironment on the continent, including almost every part of the United States, southern and western Canada, and stretches of northern Mexico. In the maritime Pacific Northwest, deer are at home in the Olympic rain forest. Inland they roam the foothills and dramatic slopes of the Cascades. Still farther to the east deer browse the high plateaus and range into the Rocky Mountains. The dry scrub of much of the American Southwest also supports surprising numbers of deer, with only arid pockets being deer free. The Midwest and East provide easy living, with stretches of clear land broken periodically by wooded sanctuaries and punctuated by rolling mountain ranges. Deer prosper farther south along the Gulf Coast and deep into the Southeast and the Florida peninsula. From river bottoms and wooded hollows to the fringes of swamps or dry slopes of chaparral, deer make themselves at home. Sometimes all that they need is a thicket along a roadside. The deer make do.

Because of their supreme adaptability, deer have not only staged the biggest comeback since country music, but in many areas their increased populations have also become a serious problem. Once humans divide and develop an area, the habitat may no longer be able to support as many deer. This leads to inevitable conflict as deer seek to survive and man seeks to enjoy his yard or his drive to work. The two species collide in more ways than one.

If Trends Persist

Natural population controls, when left alone, work with wondrous simplicity. Good conditions prompt population growth. Fawning rates are very sensitive to the health and nutrition of the mother. Plenty of high-quality forage and cover, little-to-moderate competition, and mild winters all facilitate high birth rates. In such good times over 90 percent of does bear live fawns. If conditions are *really* good, and the deer population is (or is perceived to be) low, juvenile does will mate in their first fall and produce a fawn the following spring, while mature does who otherwise commonly produce twins may give birth to triplets. The total deer population can easily double in a year.

The system works with equal efficiency when conditions are poor. Bad times mean fewer fawns will be born to compete for diminishing food supplies. Mature does produce only a single fawn; young does, none. Harsh winters wreak a heavy toll, especially if deer go into winter undernourished and in compromised health. Fawns are aborted. Deer starve to death. Predators have a heightened impact, especially if deep snow cover makes it difficult for deer to escape attacks.

Nature's system, however, is not foolproof. Inject enough folly into any system and it can break down. Deer populations can be manipulated to the brink of disaster, as evidenced by the abrupt decline in the late 1800s. But population curves can also swing to the opposite extreme. Given mild winters, no natural predators, and man-made habitats that offer plentiful food and cover, deer herds expand and expand and expand.

Management of deer populations is a complicated business. Each state has areas where populations are sustainable, other areas where the numbers are lower than optimal, and still others where overconcentration is creating problems. Problems for people. Problems for other species of wildlife. Problems for the deer themselves and the habitat. If trends persist and if deer population growth continues unimpeded in habitats that can no longer sustain such growth, we, the deer, and those habitats are in for trouble.

NATURAL HABITATS

Deer have no uniformly ideal habitat. Deer in the High Sierras, for example, have a far different habitat from those living in Philadelphia's lush suburbs. Furthermore, deer utilize their home ranges differently from year to year and from season to season.

Life on the Edge

To generalize, deer specialize in "living on the edge." Though exceptions abound, as anyone who tries to garden in some of the "nontypical" deer habitat areas can attest, deer are most often creatures of the forest edge. The forest provides cover from snow, rain, intense summer sun, and chilling winds. Deeply wooded areas also afford some respite from predators. The interwoven canopy of leafy limbs and tangled branches bars direct sunlight from reaching the ground below, which therefore can't produce adequate forage for "little woodland creatures." Without this resident food supply to

Deer typically graze
at the edge of wooded cover.

lunch on, large predators forsake such areas for more-ample pickings elsewhere. Deer, however, take advantage of this arrangement, venturing out of the woods to feed and later retreating back into the protective trees. This is why the "edge" is crucial. Deer can't eat mature trees; they can't even reach the edible parts. To prosper they must have access to open areas of fairly new growth.

The range a deer considers "home" varies. Most deer on adequate forage never travel more than one or two square miles in a lifetime, although mule deer and blacktails living at higher elevations migrate when the seasons change. Whitetails keep to the same range regardless of its condition, while deer native to sparser land must travel farther to find enough to eat. In the spring, when does give birth and bucks have not yet regrown their antlers, deer become more reclusive. By comparison, fall is a time of activity — when a young buck's thoughts turn to, well, does, and his territory expands.

Chapter Two, "Getting to Know Deer," discusses such territorial matters in greater detail.

A Brief History of Habitat Change

During the millions of years of evolution that equipped the various species and subspecies of deer to exploit virtually every type of habitat in North America (and most of the rest of the world), we can safely assume they did little to alter their environment. But then it was altered for them.

Man turned out to be a savvy predator. Not only did early Native Americans master the challenge of hunting, but they also quickly figured out some impressive wildlife management techniques. Imagine the mental lightning flash when a hunting party first realized that burned-out areas quickly resprout with fresh, tender vegetation — the favored diet of deer. So Native Americans devised a plan of simple genius: burning stretches of land to allow new growth and thereby encourage deer to stick around. This practice continued well into the twentieth century, when "more-sophisticated" land use and wildlife management techniques were adopted.

European settlers, aside from nearly annihilating the deer directly through hunting, also laid a heavy hand on habitats. Settlers kept moving farther and farther west. Cities sprang up all over what had been the heart of deer country. More recently, suburban growth has driven deer from much of what remained of their original habitat. Another ten thousand acres of habitat continue to be lost to urbanization annually.

Paradoxically, many of these otherwise catastrophic changes inadvertently benefited deer populations. As homesteaders cleared patches of land between stands of woods, they created perfect "mini-edges." Where once great forests abutted clearings and valleys, a mosaic of woodlots and farmlands emerged. Timbering contributed to opening up deep forests and introducing early succession plants — young trees, shrubs, and native ground cover. Utility companies cut vast swaths of land to erect and maintain power lines, again creating endless ribbons of new growth bordered by woodlands. Clear-cut logging operations opened up vast stretches of land once dominated by heavy timber. Edges upon edges! If it weren't for this restructuring of so much previously uninviting habitat, primarily in northern areas, the deer may never have had the success they did at reestablishing their devastated populations.

Not all deer retreated as rural development, towns, and suburbs advanced. Instead, they gradually began to blend into these unnatural habitats. As a result, their numbers have expanded to where there are often far too many deer trying to subsist in far too limited an area. Once the deer consume all the vegetation within their primary habitats, they move into new feeding grounds. Farms. Parks. Golf courses. Yards and gardens. And once they make this transition, they stay. This is what many gardeners are experiencing now, too many deer in artificial habitats. But these "feeding grounds" are limited in

Why Elk Retreated

Not all species proved as adaptable as deer. Their cousins the elk once populated the North American continent from the Carolinas to the Pacific Coast. But due to the constant encroachment of one particularly aggressive nonnative species, *Homo sapiens,* the elk retreated. They literally headed for the hills.

Now, the vast herds of elk recorded by Lewis and Clark and Teddy Roosevelt have receded into vestiges of what they once were. The lack of forage in their adopted homelands has prompted winter feeding programs for great herds of elk in such places as the National Elk Refuge at Jackson Hole, Wyoming, and the Oak Creek Wildlife Refuge in Naches, Washington. Only when the mountains are covered in snow and there is no food do the elk migrate down from the high country by the thousands, gather around feeding stations, and await their handouts like domestic cows.

how many deer they can (or will) support, and when the food runs out deer often face slow death through starvation.

In recent years one more culprit has caused changes in deer habitat, and that is the deer itself. Rare plants are being eaten out of existence. The overbrowsing in some regions has become so severe that it actually impedes the regrowth of vegetation, leaving the deer nothing to eat and nowhere to hide. The deer have eaten themselves out of house and home. Research by wildlife biologists also indicates that the deer are damaging the habitats of other wildlife that depend on low-growing vegetation for food or shelter, from woodchucks to native species of songbirds. We have affected the deer so powerfully that their counterresponse is proving deleterious not only to us, but to other species as well.

"I now suspect that just as a deer herd lives in mortal fear of its wolves, so does a mountain live in mortal fear of its deer. And perhaps with better cause, for while a buck pulled down by wolves can be replaced in two or three years, a range pulled down by too many deer may fail of replacement in as many decades."

Aldo Leopold, *A Sand County Almanac*, 1949

AT HOME ON *YOUR* RANGE

Because deer can claim just about any environment as a suitable habitat, it may seem impossible to avoid deer claiming *your* land. However, even though deer are found just about everywhere, they present a *problem* in fewer areas. And in those areas where they have become a nuisance, the degree of damage varies enormously. Gardeners in suburbs around many New England towns, for instance, are suffering real financial and emotional damage. Their yards are not merely nibbled, but ruined overnight. Deer strip shrubs of foliage from ground level to six feet high. They devour perennials and borders down to the ground. In contrast, in my area of western Washington State deer constantly come and go, and though some folks complain about a raid now and then, the damage is usually more annoying than devastating.

Your Backyard Habitat

The probability that deer will become a nuisance in your yard depends on several things. Unfortunately, the average gardener has no control over the major factors. The density of the local deer population has the greatest effect on whether or not deer become backyard pests. If the outlying areas can't support them, the deer *will* come looking. A hard winter will also drive deer to search for food. Habits of deer in the area can be particularly hard to overcome. If they have already added your garden to their menu map, you will have a tougher time discouraging their visit than if they had never discovered it. But while these are things you cannot change, you *are* in control of what kind of habitat your yard offers these ranging deer.

Compare your yard to the preferred deer habitat. Does it offer an edge? Do you have shrubs and trees for deer to browse and to use as cover? Is there a brushy or wooded area nearby? Does your yard feature a variety of plants that entice the deer? (More on which plants lure deer in Chapter Four.) Deer have definite food preferences and, having learned the difference, will forsake wild forage for tasty garden favorites anytime. The millions of Americans who enjoy feeding birds have also contributed to the deer dilemma, for the very plantings and garden arrangements that attract birds constitute an open invitation to deer. If your yard looks like a mini–game preserve, you may want to rethink your landscaping in order to avoid deer damage.

If You Want Deer Near

Many of us still truly enjoy seeing deer around our homes. The quiet, graceful movements, the soulful, liquid brown eyes, the regal yet gentle appearance, the wildness, all make deer seem somehow romantic and intriguing. We love to watch them, to reassure ourselves that there's still a place for the wild things of this world.

If you perceive deer coming close to, or perhaps into, your yard as more of a gift than a threat, then by all means maintain some of those features that deer find inviting. A dense thicket of trees and shrubs, preferably native plants, at one end of the property will make deer feel safer and therefore more welcome. An area left to native plants, a wild garden, will also appeal to deer and other backyard wildlife. Deer take in moisture from browsing on leaves or eating snow, but birdwatchers report that they will also drink from a birdbath. If you live in an area that receives heavy snowfall but offers little cover, you may even consider erecting a shelter for the deer to use in harsh weather. A simple lean-to, with the opening facing away from prevailing winds (and preferably toward a window of your home so you can watch the deer), will be appreciated.

You *can* invite deer near without encouraging damage, but be realistic. Once deer have discovered your hospitality, expect them to take advantage of it. Perhaps more than you intend. But if you, like me, are determined to have the best of both worlds, then be prepared to protect your plants. There are many ways to keep deer feeding within bounds, or at least to keep damage to a minimum. And unless their numbers are just too great or the deer are starving, you *can* have it all.

"I round a corner of the cliff and there's a doe and her fawn not ten yards away, browsing on the cliffrose. Eating flowers. . . . I breathe out, making the slightest of movements, and the doe springs up and away as if bounced from a trampoline, followed by the fawn. Their sharp hooves clatter on the rock.

" 'Come back here!' I shout. 'I want to talk to you.' "

Edward Abbey,
Desert Solitaire, 1968

If You Don't Want Deer Near

If the thought of "agent orange on hooves" visiting your garden hardly sounds "romantic and intriguing," then chances are you would just as soon deer don't come anywhere near your yard. There is hope for you, too.

Take a moment to survey your property. Identify which features may be tempting to deer. You can replace that tasty yew with a privacy fence or, alternatively, remove it and open up the area. That could make the ever-wary deer feel more exposed, more vulnerable to predators. Look for untidy or unkempt areas, which always draw wildlife. Keep all piles of brush or debris cleaned up, trees pruned, and wild grassy or weedy areas mown. This will offer less natural forage while also leaving the area more open. Learn which garden plants deer prefer (see Chapter 4) and avoid them.

There are many other tactics, discussed in further chapters, to keep deer from making themselves at home on your range. And again, unless the deer pressure in your area surpasses what the outlying habitat can support, you *can* keep the deer out.

Getting to Know Deer

Deer are extraordinarily adaptable creatures, both as individuals and as a family. In some people's estimation, their ability to adjust to any given set of circumstances is second only to that of rats. Their versatility spans ingenious behavioral adaptations as well as physical evolution. This is not good news to gardeners trying to deal with them. How, then, does one even begin to limit their comings and goings through the garden? The first step is to get to know them.

SURVIVAL IN THE WILD

People tend to have one-dimensional perceptions of deer. Some see an image of ethereal grace, velvety spirits that fade in and out of the wild wood to honor us with fleeting glimpses of their august beauty. Others find them intolerable nuisances, rats on hooves, or regard them simply as the spoils of the game, trophies to attest to one's hunting skills. And then there are those of us who admire them in their natural state, enjoy their presence, tolerate minimal damage, eat venison on occasion, and don't faint at the sight of buckskin.

Face it. Deer are not one-dimensional creatures. They are not "Bambi"s. They are not simply garden pests. They are far from "velvety spirits." Deer are flesh-and-bone wild animals whose struggle to survive is a daily life-and-death drama.

Through the aeons nature has endowed deer with an eclectic assortment of wondrously effective traits, most of them adaptations to detect and avoid predators. From the tips of their ears to the points of their hooves, deer are engineered to escape attack from natural enemies that include cougars, bobcats, bears, lynx, wolves, and even eagles.

SENSE OF SMELL. Their first line of defense is a big, wet nose — eight times bigger than that of a human, three times larger than that of most dogs. Deer rely heavily on their ability to detect and evaluate scent. A deer's sense of smell is also crucial for finding and identifying food, following deer trails, and recognizing its young.

SENSE OF HEARING. Another major asset is superior hearing, which, like their ability to smell, far exceeds that of humans. Their big ears flex and rotate constantly to detect every sound, near or far, as high pitched as a "silent" dog whistle, as quiet as the crushing of a dry leaf underfoot.

SENSE OF SIGHT. Eyesight is also important to deer. Large, prominent eyes register the slightest movement, even in dim light, thanks in part to a tapetum that reflects and thereby

Sniffing the Breeze

Many variables affect scent detection, including wind, temperature, and especially moisture. Scent reading requires some humidity, with 50–70 percent being ideal. High humidity makes deer nervous because the air is loaded with competing scents.

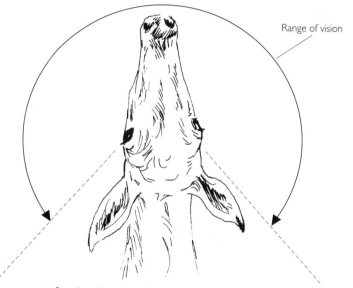

Range of vision

The placement of a deer's eyes allows it to scan roughly 270 degrees.

doubles the amount of light available to the retina. The placement of the deer's eyes on its head allows for roughly a 270-degree field of vision: binocular (both eyes focusing) in the front, monocular in a wide arc on the sides and toward the back of the head. However, in an apparent evolutionary trade-off for superior night vision, deer do not as readily detect *motionless* objects, and their perception of color is also limited. The deer's eye is loaded with rod cells, which function in low light, but has very few cone cells, which bring images into sharp focus and register color.

SPEED. A deer's best defense against predators is to run. It has been said that a deer doesn't have to outrun the predator, just the other deer. When a deer's internal alarm goes off, its long legs, powered by strong muscles built for quick bursts of speed, and its sturdy, cloven hooves, designed to ensure traction in a wide range of footings, launch the deer away from danger.

NATURAL CAMOUFLAGE. A deer's coat color provides additional protection. The color, which varies with the habitat and the season, helps deer blend into the background. Deer native to dry, cold, open areas tend to be lighter in color than those that inhabit warm, humid regions or areas of deep cover.

Coat Factors

- Deer undergo two complete molts each year.
- A deer's winter coat is nearly twice as dense as its summer coat, and the hairs are hollow.
- Deer shed from the head back.
- Healthy deer shed earlier than those in poorer health.
- Only bucks engage in mutual grooming of their coats.

than those that inhabit warm, humid regions or areas of deep cover. Coat colors turn duller in winter, permitting deer to fade more easily into the dreary backdrop of the season.

DEER SPECIES 101

Deer, moose, elk, and caribou are all closely related members of the "deer" family, Cervidae. While deer are found practically worldwide, there is a uniquely American genus, *Odocoileus*. Traditionally, only two species of *Odocoileus* have been recognized, white-tailed deer (*O. virginianus*) and mule deer (*O. hemionus*), with the latter currently including black-tailed deer. However, this view has recently been challenged by DNA research, which suggests that perhaps blacktails are actually a more primitive species than either of the other two. Scientists have classified thirty distinct subspecies of white-tailed deer, eleven subspecies of mule deer, two of black-tailed deer, and hybrids between these recognized groups.

There are four extant subspecies of elk (*Cervus canadensis*) and one species of moose (*Alces alces*). Of the four North American moose subspecies, the Alaskan moose (*A. a. gigas*) is the largest surviving member of the deer family.

While moose and elk are easy to distinguish from their smaller cousins, other deer species may seem very similar in appearance. There are three easy clues to their identity: geography, tails, and antlers.

GEOGRAPHY. The first eliminating factor in identifying deer in your area is your area. To some extent the Mississippi River forms a natural divide (see the distribution map on page 4). Although white-tailed subspecies inhabit both sides, no naturally occurring populations of black-tailed or mule deer exist east of the Mississippi. (There are, however, some artificially stocked reserves of nonnative species.) Mule deer occupy the western half of the continent. Blacktails are indigenous to the Pacific Northwest, British Columbia, and southern Alaska. As for elk, their range is limited to the Pacific Coast, the Rocky Mountains, and other western states, with pockets around the Great Lakes region. Moose inhabit only the northernmost reaches of the East, pockets of the northeastern Pacific Northwest, and the Rocky Mountains.

TAILS. Telltale tails are the best way of distinguishing deer once you've narrowed the possibilities down by geography. A comparatively large tail (about twelve inches long and nine inches wide) with long, white hairs on the underside and a broad white fanny patch give the white-tailed deer its name. When the tail goes up in characteristic fashion, white hairs flaring, there is no question about who the owner is. The black-tailed deer carries a smaller tail, black on the upper side, white on the underneath. The tail of the mule deer is narrow, white through the center with a black tip. Unlike whitetails, neither blacktails nor mule deer use their tails as signals. The tails of the many types of hybrids also have charac-

Tail characteristics help to distinguish whitetails (A), mule deer (B), and blacktails (C).

teristic markings. For example, blacktail–mule deer crosses have a black stripe running down the length of their tails.

ANTLERS. Antlers can help you identify deer species primarily in the summer and fall, when the rack is fully grown.

Unlike horns, which belong to the cow and goat families, antlers are shed and regrown every year, normally only on males, or bucks. The rack of a mature white-tailed buck features a main central beam with tines (side beams) growing out from it. In contrast, the racks of mule deer and blacktails fork repeatedly. To complicate matters, hybrids often have racks that combine features of both.

The size and complexity of the antlers depend on the age of the buck, whether nifty antlers run in his family, and how well he has been eating. Since a buck does not reach physical maturity before four years of age, up until then his highest nutritional demands are for growth. Once his body has developed to its full potential, excess nutrition is diverted into antler growth. From year to year the size and shape of his antlers may vary, depending on available food supplies.

A respectable rack is vital to a buck's standing in the deer community; the larger the antlers, the more dominant the buck. Their main function is for engaging rival bucks in battles for the right to breed. Often, a buck maintains his position merely by posturing and showing off his grand rack, but all-out fights do occur during the rut. Deerkeepers have long known that sawing the antlers off an aggressive buck renders him almost instantly submissive.

Whitetail antlers (left) typically grow tines from a single main beam, whereas mature mule deer and black-tailed (right) bucks grow antlers that repeatedly fork.

White-Tailed Deer

The nemesis of countless eastern gardeners is the whitetailed deer. Ever voracious. Seemingly fearless. Easily identified. Whitetails show the greatest variation in size, ranging from the tiny Florida Key deer (O. v. clavium), which averages a diminutive twenty-eight inches in height and weighs in around eighty pounds, to monster northern woodland whitetails (*O. v. borealis*) that top four hundred pounds. This variability reflects differences in climate (smaller bodies dissipate heat more efficiently, while larger bodies conserve it), genetics (subspecies are limited in their growth potential), and nutrition (not enough to eat or inferior forage impedes growth).

Whitetails, though somewhat discriminating in their taste preferences, will devour plants that most other animals, including blacktails and mule deer, leave alone. Their preferred habitat is the classic woodland edge, but forays into suburban and urban areas have become all too common.

Mule Deer

Slightly larger-bodied, on average, than the whitetail, mule deer also tend to weigh in a little heavier. The most common subspecies, the Rocky Mountain mule deer (*O. h. hemionus*), has a darker coat than the more typical medium brown. The desert mule deer (*O. h. crooki*) is another notable exception; its coat is a much paler shade of grayish tan, allowing it to blend into the surrounding desert.

Commonly called a muley, the mule deer gets its name from its huge ears. Big ears are a boon in areas where cover is scarce and predators may stalk from great distances. The ears also help to dissipate heat.

Muleys have a bounding gait, called the stott. When stotting, the deer uses all four legs to bounce and then lands on all four feet at once. This allows the deer to change direction with each bound — a handy way to avoid predators, specially designed for its preferred habitat of brushy, rough hillsides. By nature, muleys are less nervous than whitetails and more apt to confront a predator, including humans. Because they are less likely to run, they may seem relatively "tame."

Black-Tailed Deer

Native to the Pacific Coast are two subspecies of blacktailed deer, the Columbian (*O. h. columbianus*) and the Sitka

(*O. h. sitkensis*). They prefer the cover of dense vegetation that their native range provides. The Columbian is the larger of the two and the more likely to find its way into gardening territory, as the range of the Sitka blacktail is limited to the rain forests of the extreme north coast.

Both types of blacktails are smaller than muleys and most whitetails. Notorious for hiding rather than retreating, black-tails may make a home on your range for a long time before you even realize they are there.

Elk

Elk habitat is so restricted that most readers may wonder why bother mentioning them at all. Except for those who live in their wake. In 1995 the state of Washington paid out over $250,000 to farmers in compensation for damage to crops and fences, and this figure didn't take into account damage to major corporations, namely timber companies, *or* home gardeners.

Elk migrate in groups from small bands to enormous herds, and when they descend on your plot they leave it looking as though a demolition crew just ran through. Fences are knocked over and entire gardens trampled and devoured. In areas where elk are a problem, they can be a BIG problem.

Moose

A mature moose can stand over seven feet tall at the shoulder and weigh from thirteen hundred to fifteen hundred pounds, with a few straining the scales at up to eighteen hun-dred. Males sport racks of up to six feet across, weighing an average of fifty to sixty pounds. They feed primarily on browse, fir, aspen, and elder, and will eat their own weight each month. A moose in your backyard outclasses every other kind of deer problem you can imagine. They are big. They are hungry. They are rude and often cranky. Reports of moose charging people are practically commonplace. Never try to chase a moose away; he might return the favor.

Comparative Deer Family Characteristics

Deer	Average Size*	Color & Markings	Tail	Antler
Whitetails				
Bucks	160 lbs./ 40 inches tall	Belly patches, white around the eyes	Brown on top, white underneath	Single beam, multiple tines
Does	120 lbs./ 38 inches tall	Tan, cinnamon, brown; white muzzle, throat		
Mule Deer				
Bucks	200 lbs./ 42 inches tall	Dark to medium brown	Brown at top, white midsection, and black tip	Multiple forks
Does	140 lbs./ 40 inches tall			
Blacktails				
Bucks	150 lbs./ 38 inches tall	Reddish brown to tan	Black with white underside	Multiple forks
Does	115 lbs./ 36 inches tall			
Elk				
Bulls	500 to 1,000 lbs.	Deep reddish brown, shaggy mane, tan or light-colored rump patch	Small, same color	Branching tines from main beam; six points on average
Cows	400 to 700 lbs.			
Moose				
Bulls	1,500 lbs.	Light underbelly, dark brown hair with black tips	Primarily black with lighter points	Small; to six feet wide; palmate
Cows	1,300 lbs.			

* The size of deer varies with latitude and quality and quantity of food. The farther north and/or the better the food supply, the larger the deer.

UNDERSTANDING DEER BEHAVIOR

As with its physical makeup, a deer's every action is geared towards not being eaten. Finding food, mates, and its place in the social order are all secondary. Protecting your yard and garden requires an understanding of what drives these prey animals in their daily life.

How Deer Think

Except during mating season, when the procreative drive supersedes all else, deer live by the accompanying checklist. Everything a deer does, from the way it digests its food to the way it defines its territory, is designed to keep it from being devoured. Next in importance comes eating — no surprise to anyone needing this book! It also stands to reason that conserving energy and resting under cover are important parts of a deer's day.

Additionally, deer have a social ranking that is important enough for them to expend considerable hard-earned calories maintaining it. A dominant doe will physically challenge other does for the right of leadership by rearing up and thrashing them with her sharp hooves. A dominant buck, a mature buck with superior antlers and attitude to match, will fight

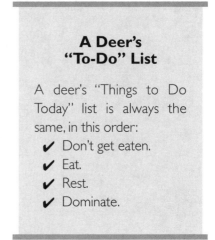

A Deer's "To-Do" List

A deer's "Things to Do Today" list is always the same, in this order:
- ✔ Don't get eaten.
- ✔ Eat.
- ✔ Rest.
- ✔ Dominate.

any buck in the woods, come mating season, for the supreme right to breed.

If the dominant deer lay a path to your door, then others will follow. Whitetails routinely follow established paths, while muleys and blacktails test the way by scent. If others have gone before, then this must be the way to go!

DEER TRUST THEIR NOSES. Glands on their bodies release various scents that deer "read" and interpret. Interdigital scent glands (between the toes) release scent wherever the deer walks. Other deer read these scent trails as the "all clear" for them to follow. A frightened deer gives off a distinct odor — other deer coming into the same area as the frightened deer, even hours later, show definite signs of distress.

DEER ARE CURIOUS, even though always on the alert. They are especially curious about unfamiliar sounds. They will often cautiously approach a new sound rather than instantly run from it.

DEER RELY ON HABIT. It seems as though deer memorize every aspect of their territory and instantly perceive anything out of place. A strange sight or smell can immediately spook deer from an area. Conversely, once deer have accepted a sight, smell, or sound, they relegate it to the "normal" category — and virtually ignore it. Deer will browse contentedly alongside highways, paying no mind to cars whizzing past, munch happily next to campgrounds amid radios blaring and children playing, even forage around military reserves during artillery practice, once they have become accustomed to these environments. Whatever association a deer learns to make with any given sight, smell, sound, or taste dictates whatever future response the deer will have to it.

DEER COMMUNICATE AND LISTEN. A lot is said through body language. The obvious example is the whitetail flag flying high and wagging from side to side in warning to other deer in the area. Deer nervous about possible danger assume a rigid posture and may stamp their front feet. Another warning signal is the snort, or sharp whistle — a shrill, sudden blast of air that sends any deer within earshot scampering. Mating season has its own body language. Deer also pay close attention to what other animals tell them. The squawk of a startled pheasant or the scolding calls of a squirrel mean just as much to the deer as to the animals that made them.

Aside from the big four on their "To-Do" list, deer have few other needs. They generally won't stray too far from natural water sources — deer need from two to four quarts of water per day — but water from stock tanks, birdbaths, garden ponds, or fountains may suffice. Deer also favor salt or mineral deposits, including that salt block your neighbors put out for their kids' pony. Shelter is another concern, and in severe wind, hail, snow, and heat deer will search out cover that may not meet with your approval. During the winter of 1988 we found four deer huddled beneath a pickup canopy that had been placed on blocks.

Now that you have a clearer understanding of how deer view their world, more needs to be said about how they end up in your yard. For that, we must consider dietary requirements and territorial imperatives in greater detail.

Diet and Digestion

Deer are actually picky eaters. When they can afford to be. Though they can eat over five hundred kinds of plants, deer will hold out for their favorites when they can find them. Each day an average-sized adult deer eats approximately seven pounds of leaves, stems, buds, blades, and other forage. An adult elk will consume three to four *times* that much, and a moose, up to 50 pounds daily. That's a lot of landscaping.

The deer's diet affects everything else in its life. An exceptional diet develops large-bodied, robust deer, prompts does to routinely twin or sometimes even bear triplets, and produces on bucks some of the most magnificent antlers imaginable. An adequate diet will keep deer alive, enable does to conceive and bear a fawn or two, and allow bucks to grow a moderate set of antlers. Malnourishment results in reduced fawning rates, underdeveloped antlers, susceptibility to disease, and, in extreme cases, starvation. It also forces deer to adapt their behavior and take serious risks in order to find food. Once deer learn where the food

> Though they can eat over five hundred kinds of plants, deer will hold out for their favorites whenever they can find them.

is, perhaps your hybrid tea rose garden, they make a habit of returning.

Deer feed and digest their food in keeping with their prime directive, "Thou shalt not get eaten." They feed mostly during low-light hours, at dawn and dusk. Their eyes are well adapted to changing light levels, while the eyes of most predators, including man, take as much as an hour to adjust. They eat "on the run" — a nibble here, a bite or two there, and then they move on. Sometimes just a few steps, sometimes a greater distance, but they don't feed in one spot for long. Deer also make a habit of feeding near some form of cover, whether it be a brush pile, forest, tall grass, or merely a slight depression in the ground that may help to hide them from view. Usually they will eat facing the prevailing wind in hopes of catching any threatening scent in time to flee.

Deer belong to a suborder of animals called ruminants, along with cattle, sheep, goats, and camels. They have a four-chambered stomach, which allows them to fill up in about an hour or two. They can then regurgitate and chew their cud in peace and quiet. This greatly reduces the time spent in the open, potentially exposed to predators.

Territorial Limits

A buck may share or overlap his territory with other bucks, while does tend to live in or near extended families of their own female fawns. Deer do tend to stay within a limited range, although whitetails tend to "yard up," or congregate, in winter, and seasonal weather patterns routinely force mule deer and blacktails, as well as elk, to migrate from the high mountains to lower feeding grounds and back again.

A deer's territory is bounded more by habit than anything else, for even in the absence of any physical barrier, little will tempt a deer from its home range. That's most likely because if doing something or going somewhere the first time didn't get it eaten, then it's likely to be safe a second time, and so on. Familiar is as close to safe as it gets for a deer. Not surprisingly, keeping to the same territory is the main reason deer tend to raid the same gardens repeatedly: The gardens are in "their" territory.

The amount of land that constitutes a deer's home range primarily depends on the forage and cover available and on the number of deer in the vicinity. For instance, mule deer in the scrublands of Arizona and New Mexico must travel farther to find sufficient food than whitetails in the rich farmlands of Illinois. In good forage deer average a one- to two-square-mile territory, usually in a roughly elliptical pattern. If food is scarce or population density high, they will roam much farther.

Natural and man-made boundaries can also determine where deer range. Distinct subspecies, such as the Hilton Head Island whitetail (*O. v. hiltonensis*) and the Blackbeard Island whitetail (*O. v. nigribarbis*), have developed on islands, where the dividing waterways provided a natural barrier. In some places major highways or urban developments form boundaries that limit deer territories.

Rogue Bucks

Romanticized though it has been, the story of the rogue buck, vigorously defending his territory against all comers, is fiction. Bucks do not maintain exclusive ranges. Their territories frequently overlap, and except during rut, there is little reason for conflict.

Getting to Know You

There is a big difference between the deer of wild country and suburban adaptees. Deer in the wild will flee at the mere whiff of human scent on a breeze. Deer in more urban areas will pull laundry off the line, steal food from picnic tables, and make themselves at home in yards, patios, even carports. Having become accustomed to the sight, sounds, movements, and smells we make, these suburbanites have lost their fear of mankind. To them we are "normal."

Deer that don't fear humans prove more of a nuisance than those we can scare away. They are certainly bolder when it comes to inviting themselves into our yards, gardens, and homes. I've seen mule deer come right up to a sliding glass door and stretch their heads inside to beg for bread. But they are still wild animals and can do considerable damage to themselves and their immediate surroundings if they panic and try to escape.

Perhaps the most ominous aspect of deer losing their natural fear of humans is that they may become aggressive. A mule deer buck typically will hesitate in order to gauge an opponent, and if he decides he "can take him" will charge rather than retreat. Worse yet is the buck or bull in rut: No unarmed human should ever challenge a buck in rut.

SEASONAL ADJUSTMENTS

Changes in the season force definite changes in the daily routine of deer life. For the gardener these behavioral adjustments mean a change of challenges.

Changes of Diet

The best diet for deer is a varied diet. They will naturally seek out a variety of plants to eat, even if an entire field of one kind of highly nutritious food, such as alfalfa, is available. They prefer plants growing in rich soil or those that are fertilized. Their "protein tooth" makes nitrogen-fixing plants, such as peas, beans, and other legumes, prime targets for garden raids.

In spring, when tender new sprouts are plentiful, deer consume mainly forbs and grasses, including such cultivated crops as winter wheat, alfalfa, and clover, and peas in home gardens. The onset of summer prompts some dietary changes as plants begin to mature and flower or fruit, but broadleaf forbs are the main item on the menu. As summer wears on, deer tend to favor broad leaves of trees, legumes, peas, beans, and corn (until the tassel ripens). Strawberries and peaches are special favorites. In the autumn, grains, berries, and fallen leaves are plentiful. Acorns, especially prized by whitetails and blacktails, litter the base of oak trees and can be detected by smell even beneath a layer of leaves or new-fallen snow. By autumn, plants are tougher and less palatable, and the deer branch out into evergreen boughs and practically anything else within reach. Cultivated crops, such as alfalfa, apples, soybeans, winter wheat, and the diversity offered by home gardens, constitute welcome additions to the diet as deer try to put on enough weight to see them through the coming hardship of winter.

Winter is the hardest on deer, particularly in northern zones. Food is scarce and the quality low; only about 10 percent of what deer can find to eat is digestible. Though they browse on dead leaves, twigs, bark, and evergreen boughs when possible, they can literally starve to death with a full stomach.

Deer become all the more aggressive in their feeding habits when there is less available. *What constitutes a nonfeeding item during the lushness of spring may become a preferred food under the poverty of winter.* Luckily, most plants can sustain the damage better if nibbled during this dormant period.

Spring Ahead

As in all of nature, spring is a time of renewal for deer. Fawns are born and nursed. Antlers on bucks begin to grow. Shaggy winter coats molt, to be replaced by sleek spring finery.

Spring Variables

- Florida whitetail bucks begin antler growth about a month ahead of northern bucks. The longer daylight hours trigger an increase in testosterone, spurring antler growth.
- Desert mule deer grow antlers about two months later than other deer. Geared toward desert cycles, antler growth depends more upon moisture than day length.

Orphans?

New fawns have no odor of their own, and does, to prevent predators from finding their young via their own scent, routinely leave new fawns alone from early morning until evening, bedded down in a safe place. There they wait until mama returns for the eight o'clock feeding. They are not abandoned, as people have the peculiar habit of thinking, and should be left alone. Wild does *may,* however, abandon fawns that have human scent on them.

Surviving deer often emerge from winter in a state of near starvation and are anxious to regain lost weight. This bodybuilding requires lots of high-protein fuel, and deer feed voraciously.

Elk, mule deer, and blacktails that had migrated to lower ground the previous winter now head back toward higher elevations. "Yards" of whitetails break up and the deer resume their normal territories. If your garden is in the path of these seasonal movements, it may become a prime stopover as tender, tempting new plants emerge from the soil.

Deer are reclusive in springtime. Pregnant does become restless and seek out a nursery territory, which they aggressively protect until their new fawns are about two months old. Except in the extreme Southwest and Southeast, most does give birth in May or June, typically to twins. But first the does chase away last year's fawns. These confused young deer are likely to turn up anywhere, including your yard and the highway. Watch out for misplaced yearling deer in the late spring.

Bucks stay in a limited area and are active for shorter periods of time, usually after dark. Their growing antlers are soft and loaded with blood vessels and sensitive nerve endings. The antlers grow quickly, about half an inch per day. Bucks know how easy it is to damage these immature status symbols and are reluctant to risk hurting themselves, so they take it easy and hide out.

Under normal conditions, does usually bear twins, which they continue to shelter until the following year.

The Good Old Summertime

Summertime and the living is easy — comparatively. Food is plentiful, at least in areas where the deer don't overwhelm the habitat, and, though not as rich as springtime fare, still nourishing. Fawns grow, learn to eat greens, and play. By the first of August, antlers reach their full growth and begin to harden, lessening the nutritional demand on the buck's body. By late August bucks begin the ritual of assaulting small trees, both to remove the dead, itchy velvet that once nourished the growing antlers and to brush up on their combat skills. Trees skinned of their bark are a sign that deer are near.

Summer is not without its vexations. The dense, short, solid hairs of the reddish brown summer coat protect the skin from sunlight and insect bites, but bugs nevertheless plague deer in hot months. If water is available, deer will plunge in to avoid them. To escape summer heat, deer become more active at night and head for cover during the daylight hours.

Autumn Daze

Because of the timing, we could say that deer "fall" in love. Or at least in lust. During the late autumn — mid-

November for most of the United States, later in warmer areas (but year-round in tropical climes) — does come into estrous beginning when they are about a year and a half old. The period in which they are receptive to breeding lasts only about twenty-four hours during this cycle. Compound this with the fact that most does come into heat within a few days of each other, and it's easy to see why bucks go a little nuts.

Only dominant bucks have the right to breed, this having been established over the summer and early fall through jousting matches and displays of machismo. They drive themselves mercilessly in their search for just the right doe on just the right day, leaving dozens of scrapes and scent markers throughout their now greatly expanded territory; lusting bucks may patrol five times their usual range. They make the rounds of these markers constantly. A breeding buck loses from 20 to 30 percent of his body weight chasing does and keeping subordinate bucks away — this just prior to the onset of winter, a time when he can least afford it.

Testosterone levels soar and bucks in rut, wild and wily, can become dangerously aggressive. They are, in fact, more dangerous just before they begin to breed than they are in the thick of it. Bucks have been known to kill other bucks,

By late summer bucks have begun rubbing off the velvet from their antlers.

In a Rut

How can you recognize a potentially dangerous buck? In most regions the first indicator is the time of year, but there are also plenty of visual signals. Serious contenders for dominance sport serious antlers. Consider any buck with more than a set of spikes as a contender. Add a dark face to the criteria to watch out for. Glands on the forehead produce an oily substance that stains the faces of dominant bucks when they rub and battle against tree trunks.

As a buck goes into rut his neck swells, making him look like a woodland linebacker. Bucks will often flare their neck hairs to make their necks look even bigger. When a buck is really looking for trouble, his hair stands on end all over his body, making him look bigger and his coat darker. He will tuck in his chin and give his opponent a hard, wide-eyed look, ears flat back against his neck, antlers tipped towards his rival. In his anger he licks his nose and flicks his tongue constantly. An angry deer's stance is rigid and he walks stiffly. He *looks* mad. Note that both elk and moose exhibit similar rutting behavior.

Because a buck in rut may choose even otherwise unappetizing trees and shrubs as sparring partners, you should take additional precautions to protect trees and shrubs from damage.

A potentially aggressive buck during rut can be distinguished by neck thickness, flared hair, darker coat, and aggressive posture.

though rarely, in dominance battles. But they have gored pets, livestock, and people to death and should never be approached indiscriminately during rut, which lasts seven to eight weeks in the North, longer in the South.

Surviving Winter

As winter nears, deer scrounge for anything that looks fattening. Winter food holds little nutrition, and a thick layer of fat is a deer's best insurance that it will live to see another spring. Its next most pressing need is to stave off the cold. A change of coats from the reddish brown of summer to the duller grayish brown of winter allows for comfort as well as camouflage. The long, hollow hairs of the grayish winter coat hold body heat in close to the skin and provide excellent insulation. The darker color even aids in absorbing what little heat the winter sun provides.

The approach of winter pushes deer to seek refuge. Elk, mule deer, and blacktails move down from high mountain feeding grounds in a mass exodus. Whitetails gather together, or "yard up," perhaps for the protection many eyes, ears, and noses can afford. Many feet also pack down snow, making it easier for them to move around.

Now weather becomes the biggest enemy. Windchill can make the cold unbearable, and unsurvivable. Deer seek out south-facing slopes to feed or rest, turning themselves into little solar collectors. During snowstorms, deer bed down and don't stir until the storm passes, even if that means waiting it out for days. Moose need deep, soft snow as insulation — when they bed down they envelop their big bodies in the snow.

Snow multiplies the dangers of being a deer. Food becomes even more scarce, with twigs, bark, and dead plants buried beneath the snow. Evergreen boughs blown down by windstorms make welcome treats. Although deer will paw through several inches of snow for food, there is a limit. Eight inches or more usually discourages them from even trying, but they can sniff out some foods — apples, acorns, corn — under a foot of snow. Worse yet, snow makes it harder to move around; the deer's sharp hooves were designed for solid ground, not snow-shoeing. Pushing through snow burns more calories at a time when the deer has none to spare, and its markedly slower movements give predators a seemingly unfair advantage.

As winter wears on, starvation begins to take its toll. Twigs and bark are stripped from ground level to as high as the deer can reach when standing on its back legs. Deer prefer smaller twigs, those no bigger than a wooden matchstick, and if larger twigs are being consumed, take it as a sign that the deer in your area are starving. If water isn't available, they will eat snow, which burns extra calories, furthering the progress of starvation. Deer become weaker and less active. If the winter is severe enough, unborn fawns may be aborted or resorbed by the mother's body. Starvation gives diseases and parasites an open door and can compromise the digestive system to the point that nourishment cannot be processed.

A starving deer stands with its back arched against the cold. If it can walk, it may stagger and fall. Its eyes are dull, its coat rough, its bones protrude through the dense hair. And when there is one such suffering animal, there are more. No longer the magnificent embodiment of grace and wild beauty, starving deer can only wait. For spring, if it comes in time, for death if it doesn't. Though deer have been known to survive up to a month or two with *no food whatsoever*, it is not unusual for up to half of a given deer population to die in winter.

Winter Reversal

Unlike most other warm-blooded animals, deer experience a slowing of their metabolic rate as temperatures drop. Virtually all growth stops as maintenance becomes the goal.

Antlers, solid bone that could slash an opponent to pieces one day, suddenly dimineralize and simply drop off. The deer become sedentary, a life-saving state under the conditions.

What Are the Damages?

As we have seen, because people and deer share more and more of each other's habitat, deer damage has become a serious issue. Each year millions of gardens, thousands of vehicles, and untold numbers of pets and people are affected by deer being in the wrong place at the wrong time.

Sometimes deer, and more often elk or moose, can do considerably more damage than just knocking down fences as they pass through your property. Many a rural homeowner has been roused during the night to chase after errant livestock set free by fence-smashing deer. Sometimes the damage isn't discovered until later, sometimes with serious consequences.

GARDEN DAMAGE

Right now, out there somewhere, a deer is gobbling down someone's prize posies or hard-earned produce. The estimated annual loss of crops, garden, and landscaping runs into hundreds of millions of dollars nationwide. Deer damage a wide assortment of crops, vegetables, fruit trees, nursery stock, and ornamental landscape plantings. The damage is not only immediate but also long-term, reducing yields in crops or fruit trees and permanently destroying ornamentals and nursery stock.

Because deer tend to eat on the move, moderate garden raids need not be all that damaging to the plants. Most trees and shrubs can sustain some browsing and still survive. The true damage is ultimately revealed when the growth of the plant is altered. Removal of terminal and lateral buds from shrubs and trees causes them to change their normal growth pattern. Often, squat, bushy shrubs and stunted trees result.

Damage to plants is not limited to feeding. From September through November, when the velvet dies from their antlers, bucks aggressively rub against small trees — those with trunks less than six inches in diameter — and shrubs to remove it. As the deer joust with the hapless vegetation the velvet is peeled away, the antlers sharpened and polished. Bucks get downright zealous, rubbing and thrusting to strengthen their neck muscles and fighting skills for real battles with nonvegetative opponents. They let off steam, prepare for battle, and reduce your shrubbery to splinters. Plants beneath the chosen limbs take a beating too, as the deer's sharp hooves trample, tear, and effectively till the soil.

Heavily damaged by rubbing, broken limbs and peeled bark can permanently disfigure landscape trees and shrubs.

Deer damage is instantly evident in the home garden. You may check the garden in the evening to find all is well, only to discover disaster in the morning. Sharp hooves have crushed and shredded freshly transplanted flowers. Curious noses have overturned potted plants, probably breaking numerous clay or ceramic containers in the process. Greedy mouths have ripped foliage from limb, stem, and stalk. Every blossom from your rosebush has been devoured, while flowers from other plants were nibbled indiscriminately. Once neat rows are now staggered clumps. Your garden is a mess. And worse yet, the predators may return tomorrow night.

Scenes like this are played out all over "deer country." Of course many gardeners suffer only minor annoyances, such as a few leaves munched here and there, but others routinely endure mass havoc. It can become very expensive trying to overcome deer and still maintain landscaping or a garden. Replanting costs for mature ornamentals are premium. Many gardeners find themselves starting over season after season, never coming close to realizing the mature landscape or productive garden of their dreams.

> We garden to create our own private patch of Eden. When deer violate these living sanctuaries, they damage more than plants. They hurt us.

But the true cost of such damage goes beyond the financial or aesthetic setbacks. Most people garden, at least in part, because of the soul-deep need to connect with the earth itself, to be part of the natural process of planting, nurturing, and harvesting. We garden to create our own private patch of Eden, to renew ourselves and escape the demands of daily life. There is a true, deep, emotional investment. When deer violate these living sanctuaries, they damage more than plants. They hurt us.

INVESTIGATING THE SCENE

The first step in controlling deer damage is to positively identify the problem.

TRACKS. Left in soft soil, mud, or snow, tracks are usually a good identifier. But look closely. Elk and cow tracks are similar, though elk tracks are more pointed at the tips than those of cattle. Llamas, too, leave tracks much like those of elk. Goat tracks can look a lot like deer tracks. In relying on tracks to tell the tale, it helps to know the livestock in your area.

Deer tracks, as pictured on page 41, are usually about three inches in length. The track depends on the condition of the ground, the deer's speed, and the deer that left it. The sharper the edges of the tracks, the fresher. But mud, rain, wind, or freezing and thawing temperatures affect tracks, making them look bigger, older, or fresher than they really are. Running

Raiders of the Dark

Many years ago a resident of Woodinville, Washington, felt certain that elk were regularly ransacking her garden. Every so often she would find bean poles shoved over and trampled, entire rows of produce munched to the ground, and, most incriminating, large cloven-hoofed tracks that had churned up her carefully tended soil. The raids always happened at night, so she had not actually seen the offending creatures.

Local officials advised her that she might be able to file a claim with the state for compensation, but she would have to prove that elk were damaging her property. Determined to catch them in the act, she devised a plan. She ran twine around the perimeter of the garden, with two or three tin cans tied together at irregular intervals. Surely when the elk trespassed next time they would set off her alarm and she would have her proof.

Sure enough, three days after she set the trap, clanging cans alerted her that intruders had entered her garden. She rushed out to confront the culprits, only to find her neighbor's cow contentedly enjoying a midnight snack.

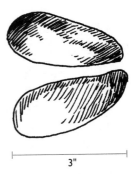

Deer tracks are about three inches long. In soft soil or thin snow cover, dewclaws of bucks may leave characteristic drag marks.

deer leave tracks much farther apart than walking, browsing, eating deer. Buck tracks are slightly wider than those left by does, and if the soil is soft (or covered by less than an inch of snow) their dewclaws will often leave characteristic drag marks. Because bucks are heavier and more active than does, they tend to wear their feet down faster and their tracks may be more rounded at the tips, but it's difficult to compare. In the summer, does often travel with their fawns, so doe tracks may be accompanied by one or two smaller sets.

SCAT. Another calling card left by deer is scat, or droppings. In late summer, fall, winter, and early spring, when a deer's diet consists mostly of browse, the droppings are small, elongated pellets. When deer feed on lush greenery or fruit, the pellets clump together in a mass. Warm and shiny droppings are fresh, meaning deer are still very near. Cool and shiny droppings are no more than a few hours old, and dull droppings could be from days ago. Bucks tend to take potty stops, while does tend to be constantly on the move. Small piles of scat most likely point to a buck as the author, whereas scattered scat was probably the work of a meandering doe. Unfortunately, even here impostors can confound things. Rabbit droppings look much like those of deer, but are always round. Goats and llamas leave elongated pellets, similar to those of deer on browse.

DEER BEDS. The presence of deer beds also indicates that deer feel at home in or near your yard. They bed down for the day in brush or tall grass, camouflaged from potential predators. If an area seems safe to them, they will make a habit of bedding down in the general vicinity. Having found a particularly choice spot, deer may return to the same bed time after time. Packed-down, swirled sections of grass about three feet around are another sign that you are sharing your habitat with deer.

DAMAGED PLANTS. Among the best of signs, not only that deer have visited, but also that deer have in fact caused the damage, are the plants left behind. If you find leaves and twigs snipped off clean, then deer are *not* to blame (at least this time). Deer have no upper incisors. Bottom teeth meet a tough upper pad in the top of the mouth. When a deer has a mouthful it quickly pulls its head to one side to tear the food free. This leaves a characteristic jagged edge to leaves and torn stems. Rabbits, woodchucks, and the neighbor's pony will bite plants off cleanly. Deer, goats, and llamas must rip them free. In times of famine deer leave what is known as a browse line: Every green stem, bud, or twig of gnawable size gets eaten, from ground level to as high as the deer can reach

Note the jagged edge of the remaining stems. This is typical of deer damage.

when standing on their hind legs (about six or seven feet). No bunny could do that, and unless the neighborhood livestock is also starving, it's very unlikely that goats, cows, or llamas will.

Of course the best evidence that deer have caused your gardening woes is to catch them in the act. There is no more damning testimony than that of an eyewitness. During most of the year the best time to catch deer in your yard is early morning or evening. Though deer are active on and off for most of the day, they tend to reserve mealtime for the twilight hours. If in doubt, camp out.

OTHER INJURIES AND INSULTS

Not to be outdone by TV, inner-city crime, and politicians, deer have caused problems we could never have imagined until it was too late. In places where deer populations have stretched the habitat to the breaking point, confrontations with people and deer have come to an all-time high.

Direct Confrontations

Though not often, deer can and have attacked pets and people. Bucks in rut are especially unpredictable and may take their aggression out on anything that *in their perception* dares to challenge them. At least one attack in Texas left a man trampled and gored to death by a whitetail buck in rut. Another Texas attack left three surveyors shaken, but alive to tell their story. One of the workers was pitched twenty feet into the air by the raging beast.

Traffic Tragedies

Most human suffering attributable to deer is caused by accidents. An average of 120 fatalities occur annually because of collisions with deer, making deer the number one wildlife killer of man. Ironic, but nonetheless tragic. On average, three hundred thousand vehicles collide with deer every year in the United States. In 1995 the state of

Clear the Deck

A Wisconsin woman awoke one night to the frantic barking of her dog, Ernie, outside on the deck. Fast, heavy footsteps, more barking, yelping, and scurrying roused her from her bed. She rushed to the back kitchen door to see what all the commotion was about and had barely inched it open when Ernie burst in, terrified. More stamping footsteps and she flipped on the back porch light and peered through the kitchen window to see an irate buck stomping the floorboards of the deck.

Wisconsin alone reported forty thousand such collisions. Insurance agencies estimate that over $180 million in claims are paid out each year for deer-related accidents — and that figure reflects only *reported claims*. The actual cost could be several times higher, since many people never report such accidents to their insurance companies.

Of course, most of these collisions do not result in human fatalities, but the odds for the deer are not as good. Even when a deer that has been hit bounds off, apparently none the worse for the incident, the deer may, in fact, be mortally wounded. Seemingly insignificant injuries can prove life-threatening. An injured deer doesn't have much of a chance of outrunning a predator.

Grille-mounted deer whistles, designed to warn deer of oncoming traffic, have been touted by many, including insurance companies, as a means to prevent collisions with deer. Others have their doubts since the whistle's effective range is narrow and directly forward. Deer can't hear it unless they are standing directly in front of it, in the path of the oncoming vehicle.

Strange Encounters

Deer can turn up in some pretty unusual places. Reports abound of deer turning up in busy metropolitan areas, stopping traffic and startling the citizenry. One deer that found its way into downtown Washington, D.C., had to be darted and removed.

Deer are phenomenal swimmers and can keep afloat for long periods of time, especially in winter, when their hollow-haired coats cause them to ride higher in the water. Good thing. There are innumerable reports of deer falling into swimming pools and other man-made water hazards and needing help to get out. The vertical sides of pools make it impossible for the deer to climb out on their own. Not all survive.

Steering Clear

Following these suggestions may help you avoid colliding with deer on the road:

- Drive more carefully during twilight hours.
- Realize that spring and fall are peak times of deer activity, and exercise more caution.
- Be aware of the surrounding terrain. Remember that deer prefer "edge" habitats.
- Heed deer-crossing signs. They are there for a reason — slow down and stay alert!
- Watch for eyes. Deer's eyes reflect lights and will glow at you from the side of the road. Slow down or stop when you spot them.
- If one deer crosses the road in front of you, be prepared for a second. Does usually travel in pairs or small groups.

If you do happen to hit a deer, report it to your local game authorities (anonymously, if you prefer).

Breaking In, Breaking Out

Glass is not a concept deer understand. Reports of deer crashing through windows or plate glass doors are more common than those who live in glass houses would care to think about. Once inside, the confused creature predictably panics and tears the place apart.

In one case near Philadelphia, the homeowner was gone when a four-point buck barged in. Neighbors rallied to rid the house of the intruder. Breaking open another window as an escape route and opening the door, police and neighbors banged against the sides of the house to shoo the deer out. Suddenly onlookers were treated to more than they had expected when the deer burst through the broken-out window and charged directly toward them. Spectators and deer all beat a hasty retreat.

Though no one can prevent all freak accidents, you can at least attempt to protect your property, and the deer. Be sure to fence all pools (eight feet high to deter deer) or cover them when not in use. Make large windows more visible by placing stickers on them or by drawing shades, curtains, or blinds, especially during the times when deer are most active. Never tempt a deer to come indoors — neither of you will enjoy the encounter.

HEALTH CONCERNS

No list of deer worries would be complete without mentioning some of the health issues that involve deer. Lyme disease, particularly in the eastern United States, has become a serious public health concern. In much of New England, virtually everyone knows of someone who has had Lyme disease. Nationally, doctors reported thirteen thousand new cases in

1994, a 60 percent jump over the previous year. Caused by the spirochete *Borrelia bugdorferi*, Lyme disease is transmitted by a tick, *Ixodes scapularis*, loosely referred to as the deer tick despite being much more prevalent in deer *mice*. Many victims never even notice the tick or the bite. Those infected characteristically develop a ring-shaped rash and flulike symptoms, including fatigue, chills, fever, aches, and headaches, within a week to ten days. Though easily cured in the early stages with tetracycline, Lyme disease can lead to serious complications if left untreated.

While it's easy to blame the deer, they don't carry the disease. The ticks do. And researchers have discovered that cats, dogs, cows, and a variety of other wildlife, including foxes, raccoons, skunks, and rabbits, also host the ticks.

Two additional tick-borne diseases require mention. Human babesiosis, caused by the parasite *Babesia microti*, is a malaria-like infection that was first diagnosed in the United States on Nantucket Island, Massachusetts, in the 1970s. It can be transmitted along with Lyme disease when a tick feeds, and though many victims never show symptoms, it is potentially fatal. Severe to fatal cases occur in people with weakened immune systems, especially those without an intact

Avoiding Lyme Disease

To avoid being bitten and infected:
- ◆ Wear insect repellent containing deet whenever you venture outdoors in deer tick territory.
- ◆ Wear long pants and a long-sleeved shirt when possible.
- ◆ If Lyme disease is endemic in your area, consider having your yard treated for ticks. Product tests estimate that yards treated with Damminix Lyme Disease Control, a biodegradable product, have 97 percent fewer suspect ticks than untreated yards.

spleen. Symptoms, including anorexia, fatigue, fever, sweats, chills, headache, and nausea, usually develop from one to four weeks after a tick bite. The telltale skin rash of Lyme disease is absent with babesiosis, which remains rare: Only a few hundred cases have been reported nationwide to date.

Human granulocytic ehrlichiosis (HGE) was recognized as a new disease in 1993, until then commonly being misdiagnosed as "rashless" Lyme disease because other symptoms are similar. About a hundred cases, including four fatalities, have been confirmed in Connecticut, Massachusetts, Minnesota, New York, Rhode Island, and Wisconsin. If diagnosed early on, HGE responds readily to tetracycline.

Other health concerns involve disease agents that can be transmitted to livestock. Among the most worrisome is the spinal meningeal worm, carried by whitetails. It is fatal to mule deer, blacktails, elk, moose, llamas, goats, and some sheep.

Deer-o-Scaping

Let's hope that the first three chapters have helped increase your understanding of deer and how they live. Possibly you've reached a vantage point from which these marvelous wild creatures merit newfound respect.

But now we need to begin applying our knowledge to this book's principal concern: how to limit deer damage to your yard and garden. The first option involves reconsidering what plants, shrubs, and trees you select for your property.

Just as Xeriscaping was developed to meet the demands of gardening with limited water, so too can the gardener establish and maintain his plot under a plan to prevent deer damage. *Deer-o-scaping*, to coin a term, can be defined as the style of gardening that incorporates plants and gardening styles designed to discourage deer damage. Deer-o-scaping depends on three things:

- Avoiding the plants deer prefer
- Taking advantage of plants deer don't like
- Incorporating garden designs that discourage deer

These can be important first steps toward thwarting the unwelcome advances of dining deer.

WHY YOUR YARD MAY LURE DEER

Gardens in very different settings draw deer. What the deer find so irresistible may have as much to do with the surrounding area as the individual yard. While there may be little you can do to change your setting, understanding the environment it provides can be very helpful in understanding what deer find so appealing about your particular plot.

Rural Garden Parties

It used to be that we automatically associated deer with a rural setting. And though they have certainly spread beyond the countryside, deer are still most common in rural areas.

Rural gardens attract deer because they offer a

> Rural gardens attract deer because they offer a neat little buffet right in the middle of the deer's domain. It's like one-stop shopping for deer.

neat little buffet right in the middle of the deer's domain. Rather than search their entire range for a suitable mix of vegetation, they find everything they could ask for in a single convenient location. It's like one-stop shopping for deer. And nearby, deer can usually find cover, water, and possibly other enticements, such as feed, salt, or mineral blocks for livestock. Deer do not fear livestock and may even be comforted by their presence. It's almost as if they think, "Gee, if these guys think it's safe to hang out here, it must be okay for us, too." A rural landscape offers less commotion, noise, and olfactory distraction, so deer naturally feel more "at home."

If you garden in a rural setting, check nearby pastures and woods for trails. Whitetails will randomly use the same trails over and over again.

Suburban Splendor

Suburban growth continues to encroach upon deer country. Newly developed 'burbs disorient deer, who have probably used the same trails to the same food sources and water for generations. The deer find themselves suddenly displaced, exposed to traffic, noise, strange fumes, and dogs. Habitat areas are reduced and fragmented, which increases the deer pressure on remaining resources. With less natural habitat and food available, deer are lured into yards well stocked with new plants. Eventually these plants may even replace the deer's normal diet.

Suburban gardens may offer deer the same food choices as rural plots, but in this setting there may be dozens of gardens within the range of each deer. If your garden also provides, or is near, brush or bushy cover, it may become a favored stopover along the deer's garden tour. Culs-de-sac and dead-end streets, in particular, often offer just the right combination of quiet, cover, and cuisine.

Urban Invitations

Despite everything that deer hold dear — bucolic surroundings, peace and quiet, an "edge," nearby water — they have increasingly become a problem in urban settings. This occurs most often in the spring, when young deer are chased away by their mothers in preparation for birthing new fawns. If these confused and inexperienced young deer survive their initial forays into strange territory and discover the rewards offered by community gardens or well-fertilized park lawns, they may return.

Deer don't generally have to make all that great an adjustment to city life. Deer that find their way downtown are not traveling down from the mountains, but commuting in from the suburbs. They will have already learned to dismiss the sights, sounds, and smells of the city. As yearling deer establish their own territories, they tend to stay close to their mothers' home range, although bucks venture farther than does. But with so many deer already inhabiting surrounding

Deer that find their way downtown are not traveling down from the mountains, but commuting in from the suburbs.

areas, each succeeding generation inches closer to urbanized settings.

Often hemmed in by highways, housing developments, or other human barriers, city deer face real challenges in finding enough to eat and a place to hide. Virtually any greenery in the city becomes a meal, and the sparsest shrubbery can provide sufficient cover. Parks often host deer until damage becomes evident. In this context, any lush, well-fertilized plants and lawns are beacons, and your city garden an oasis.

DEER FAVORITES

The first rule of deer-o-scaping is to avoid plants that deer actively seek out. As anyone who has ever broken this rule can attest, deer will make pigs of themselves when they find their favorite foods. And they will do it over and over again. A friend of mine who loves roses used to have several well-tended bushes along the walkway of her woodland home. Not anymore. Once the deer chanced upon the poor rosebushes, they devoured them. To make matters worse, the deer soon discovered other plants and the vegetable garden. Now my friend seeks out plants the deer won't eat.

Even though it may seem that deer will eat anything that holds still long enough, the fact is they have distinct preferences. Gardeners, beware: Plants on the Deer "Prefer to Eat" List should, like double butter brickle ice cream, be indulged in sparingly. These plants tempt deer into your garden when they might otherwise never set hoof inside the gate. Don't despair, however, if some of *your* favorites also happen to be on the list. There are many ways to incorporate selected plants into a deer-o-scaped yard. And, looking ahead, perhaps plant breeders could help out. Color, form, and fragrance have

A Deer "Prefer-to-Eat" List

Trees, Shrubs, Vines
Azaleas (*Rhododendron* spp.)
American arborvitae *(Thuja occidentalis)*
Apple (*Malus* spp.)
Atlantic white cedar (*Chamaecyparis thyoides*)
Balsam fir *(Abies balsamea)*
Buckeye *(Aesculus california)*
Cherry (*Prunus* spp.)
Clematis (*Clematis* spp.)
Cornelian dogwood *(Cornus mas)*
Crab apple (*Malus* spp.)
Eastern redbud *(Cercis canadensis)*
English/American hybrid yew *(Taxus baccata)*
English ivy *(Hedera helix)*
European mountain ash *(Sorbus aucuparia)*
Fraser fir *(Abies fraseri)*
Hybrid tea roses (*Rosa odorata* hybrids)
Japanese yew *(Taxus cuspidata)*
Korean lilac *(Syringa patula)*
Norway maple *(Acer platanoides)*
Peach *(Prunus persica)*
Plum (*Prunus* spp.)

Rhododendron (*Rhododendron* spp.)Vinca (*Vinca minor*)
Vine maple *(Acer circinatum)*
Western yew *(Taxus brevifolia)*
Winged euonymus *(Euonymus alata)*
Winter creeper *(Euonymus fortunei)*

Flowers and Garden Plants
Beans (*Phaseolus* spp.)
Blackberry (*Rubus* spp.)
Broccoli, cauliflower (*Brassica* spp.)
Chrysanthemum (*Chrysanthemum* spp.)
Daylilies (*Hemerocallis* spp.)
Geum (*Geum* spp.)
Hosta (*Hosta* spp.)
Lettuce (*Lactuca* spp.)
Peas (*Pisum satirum*)
Raspberry (*Rubus* spp.)
Spring bulbs (various)
Strawberry (*Fragaria* spp.)
Sweet corn *(Zea mays)*
Trillium (*Trillium* spp.)
Tulip (*Tulipa* spp.)

been accentuated by selective plant breeding, so maybe there's reason to hope for fuzzy-leaved hostas, bitter-tasting roses, and spiny-stemmed daylilies.

PLANTS DEER AVOID EATING

Nature equipped deer, like other animals, with an innate sense of what is and what isn't good for them. They will munch edible mushrooms contentedly but never nibble unsafe varieties. They may browse your browallia but forsake the foxglove. When it comes to poisonous plants, they just know. However, some plants they avoid are more like spinach on a toddler's plate — they just don't *like* them. Three things dictate which plants deer usually will *not* eat:

- The deer's previous experience with the plant. If a plant makes them sick or is associated with a bad experience, deer tend to avoid it in the future.
- The degree of hunger. If there's nothing else to eat, suddenly spinach doesn't taste so bad.
- The individual deer. (Hey, some kids *like* spinach.)

"Plants deer won't eat" is, of course, a relative category. If a deer tries an unpalatable food in the midst of plenty, it will be less likely to go for seconds. Most plant foods reach their prime in spring and early summer, becoming less tasty and tougher as they mature. However, if a normally rejected food constituted the only sustenance when starvation threatened, a deer will remember it as a good food.

Starving deer become bolder. Other instincts and fears become clouded by the need for food. They will disregard all sorts of deterrents, usually in winter when snow cover and the natural dormancy of plants make other foods unavailable, and bravely test previously untouched gardens and plants. Starvation, though, is not confined to wintertime in areas where deer overwhelm the habitat. If the deer density in your area is high enough, you may encounter starving deer anytime.

To complicate matters further, deer are very inconsistent when it comes to diet. They have preferences, but no absolutes. Except for what is downright toxic, deer don't seem to agree much on what they like and dislike. The menu changes from deer to deer, year to year, and even season to season among the same deer. As gardeners we have to work from generalities, tempered by our individual experiences.

Deer do find several things unappetizing. They usually don't eat plants with coarse, fuzzy, bristly, or spiny textures. They also shun plants with intense aromas. Some plants just taste yucky — deer have been observed taking a "test taste" and virtually spitting out offending plants.

Getting Down to Specifics

The list on pages 56–68 identifies plants least likely to be consumed or seriously damaged by deer. The list is a starting point, not a guarantee, however, because deer, whose food preferences vary from region to region, have devoured some so-called deer-proof plants (Clematis and Fraser fir, for example) in enough places that to include them inspires a false sense of security. Many plants not eaten in suburban Chicago can be deer fodder outside Dallas. Also, the list omits some plants that *are* deer resistant, because they have undesirable growth patterns, such as kudzu vine, or because they are poisonous, such as monkshood (*Aconitum* spp.).

Note that many drought-resistant plants can also be considered deer resistant, probably because of the tougher cell structure necessary to withstand desiccation, which makes them unpalatable. Always bear in mind, however, that "drought tolerance" is a quality of *established* plants. New plants introduced into your garden need sufficient watering to grow and send down their roots. During this period of tender growth they may still tempt deer. Similarly, you should consider the listed trees as deer resistant after the trees reach a reasonable level of maturity. Very young trees of almost any kind may be seriously injured by curious nibbling. Protect young trees until they outgrow the danger.

*Deer-Resistant Plants**

Name	Zone	Soil	Light
Annuals			
Ageratum, floss flower *Ageratum houstonianum*		Rich, well-drained, humusy	○◑
Borage *Borago officinalis*		Moderately rich	○
Ice plant *Mesembryanthemum crystallinum*		Poor, sandy	○
Pincushion flower *Scabiosa atropurpurea*		Well-drained	○
Pot marigold *Calendula officinalis*		Moderate to rich loam	○◑
Verbena, vervain, garden verbena *Verbena x hybrida*		Rich, light, well-drained	○◑
Zinnia *Zinnia*		Fertile, rich, well-drained	○
Perennials			
Allium *Allium* spp.	3–10	Any, well-drained (most species)	○◑
Aloe *Aloe vera*	10	Well-drained, sandy loam	○◑
Artemisia, wormwood, sagebrush *Artemisia* spp.	2–9	Any, well-drained	○
Arum lily, calla lily *Zantedeschia* spp.	10	Rich, fertile, well-drained loam	○◑
Bachelor's button *Centaurea cineraria*	6–9	Average to rich	○◑
Bellflower *Campanula* spp.	3–9	Fertile, gritty loam, well-drained	○◑
Black-eyed Susan *Rudbeckia hirta*	3–9	Average to rich, well-drained	○◑
Bleeding heart *Dicentra spectabilis*	3–8	Moderately rich, moist, well-drained	○◑
Bluebonnet, lupine *Lupinus* spp.	4–8	Llight or sandy, well-drained	○◑
Cactus *Cactaceae*	Varies	Well-drained, sandy	○

○ Full sun ◑ Part shade ● Shade

Name	Zone	Soil	Light
California fuchsia, hummingbird trumpet *Zauschneria californica*	8–10	Poor	○
Catmint, catnip *Nepeta* spp.	3–8	Moderately rich, well-drained loam	○◑
Century plant *Agave americana*	7–10	Well-drained, dry, sandy	○
Chives *Allium schoenoprasum*	3–11	Rich, moist, well-drained	○◑
Columbine *Aquilegia* spp.	3–10	Well-drained, rich in leaf mold	○◑
Daffodil, jonquil *Narcissus* spp.	3–9	Fertile, well-drained	○◑
Dame's rocket *Hesperis matronalis*	3–10	Moist, well-drained	○◑
Date palm *Phoenix dactylifera*	10	Well-drained, rich, sandy loam	○
Delphinium *Delphinium* spp.	4–7	Rich, well-drained	○◑
Dusty miller* *Senecio cineraria*	9–10	Any, well-drained	○
English lavender *Lavandula angustifolia*	5–10	Well-drained, light, sandy	○
Fennel* *Foeniculum vulgare*	6–10	Moderately rich, well-drained	○
Fern Several genera, many species	Varies	Moist, rich loam	◑●
Forget-me-not *Myosotis scorpioides*	4–10	Rich, moist to wet	○◑
Foxglove *Digitalis* spp.	4–8	Well-drained, humusy	◑●
Geranium *Geranium* spp.	5–7	Well-drained, average	○◑
Garden sage *Salvia officinalis*	5–9	Good garden soil	○
Golden marguerite *Anthemis tinctoria*	4–9	Poor, well-drained	○●
Hellebore *Helleborus* spp.	3–8	Rich, humusy	●
Iceland poppy *Papaver nudicaule*	2–9	Rich, well-drained	○
Iris *Iris* spp.	Varies	Average to rich, well-drained to wet	○◑

○ Full sun ◑ Part shade ● Shade

Name	Zone	Soil	Light
Lady's mantle *Alchemilla mollis*	3–8	Good garden soil	◐
Lamb's ears *Stachys byzantina*	4–9	Moist, sandy loam	○
Lamium, dead nettle *Lamium maculatum*	3–8	Rich, moist loam	◐●
Lily of the Nile *Agapanthus africanus*	8–10	Rich, heavy loam	○◐
Matilija poppy *Romneya coulteri*	9–10	Sandy, gravelly, well-drained	○
Mint *Mentha* spp.	4–9	Rich, moist, well-drained	Varies
New Zealand flax, New Zealand hemp *Phormium tenax*	9–10	Any	○◐
Oregano, wild marjoram *Origanum vulgare*	4–10	Poor, light, well-drained	○
Oriental poppy *Papaver orientale*	3–9	Rich, well-drained	○
Oxalis, wood sorrel *Oxalis*	Varies	Rich, moist loam	Varies
Parsley *Petroselinum crispum*	3–10	Rich, deep, well-drained	○◐
Peach leaf bellflower *Campanula persicifolia*	3–8	Light to rich	○●
Peony *Paeonia* spp.	4–9	Tolerates any, prefers rich loam	○●
Prickly phlox *Leptodactylon californicum*	9–10	Sandy, gravelly	○
Pride of Madeira *Echium candicans*	8–10	Well-drained	○
Red valerian, Jupiter's beard *Centranthus ruber*	5–7	Rich, well-drained	○◐
Rose campion *Lychnis coronaria*	4–10	Well-drained, fertile	○
Rosemary *Rosmarinum officinalis*	6–10	Light, well-drained	○◐
Russian sage *Perovskia atriplicifolia*	4–9	Well-drained	○
Saint-John's-wort *Hypericum* spp.	4–10	Dry, light	◐
Santolina *Santolina chamaecyparissus*	6–9	Any	○

○ Full sun ◐ Part shade ● Shade

Name	Zone	Soil	Light
Snapdragon* *Antirrhinum majus*	8–10	Average to rich, well-drained	○◑
Snowflake *Leucojum* spp.	4–10	Average, well-drained	◑
Tansy *Tanacetum vulgare*	3–10	Rich, well-drained	○
Thyme *Thymus* spp.	4–10	Light, sandy, well-drained	○●
Yarrow *Achillea* spp.	3–9	Well-drained, moist to dry	○◑

* Commonly grown as an annual in colder regions

Ornamental Grasses

Name	Zone	Soil	Light
Bamboo Several genera; many species	Varies	Fertile, moist, well-drained	Varies
Blue fescue *Festuca glauca*	4–7	Poor, sandy, dry	◑
Eulalia grass *Miscanthus sinenis*	4–9	Rich, moist	○
Lemon grass *Cymbopogon citratus*	9–10	Average garden soil	○
Pampas grass *Cortaderia selloana*	8–10	Any, well-drained	○

Shrubs & Trees

Name	Zone	Soil	Light
Acacia, wattle Joshua tree, yucca *Acacia*	9–10	Good, moist, well-drained	○
Adam's needle *Yucca* spp.	Varies	Well-drained, sandy	○◑
American persimmon *Diospyros virginiana*	4–9	Well-drained garden soil	○
American sweet-gum *Liquidambar styraciflua*	5–9	Fertile, moist, slightly acid	○
Ash *Fraxinum* spp.	3–9	Varies	○
Australian fuchsia *Correa* spp.	9–10	Dry, well-drained	○◑
Barberry *Berberis* spp.	4–8	Varies	○◑
Beefwood *Casuarina verticillata*	9–10	Any	○
Black locust *Robinia pseudoacacia*	3–8	Any, well-drained	○

○ Full sun ◑ Part shade ● Shade

Name	Zone	Soil	Light
Bottle tree *Brachychiton populneus*	9–10	Average, dry	○
Box elder *Acer negundo*	2–9	Moist, fertile to dry, poor	○
Boxwood *Buxus*	Varies	Any, well-drained	○◑
Bridal veil broom *Retama* (formerly *G. monosperma*)	9–10	Well-drained	○
Brush cherry *Syzgium paniculatum*	9–10	Varies	○
Bush cinquefoil *Potentilla fruticosa*	2–7	Rich to poor, well-drained	○◑
Bush germander *Teucrium fruticans*	8–10	Poor, gravelly	○
Butterfly bush *Buddleia* spp.	5–10	Fertile, well-drained	○
California laurel, myrtle *Umbellularia californica*	8–10	Moist	○●
California pepper tree, pepperwood *Schinus molle*	8–10	Sandy, well-drained	○
California sweet shrub *Calycanthus occidentalis*	6–10	Fertile	○◑
Cape leadwort *Plumbago auriculata*	9–10	Sandy, well-drained	○
Carolina cherry laurel *Prunus caroliniana*	7–10	Moist, well-drained	○◑
Cascades mahonia *Mahonia nervosa*	5–8	Average garden soil	○◑
Chinaberry tree *Melia azedarach*	7–10	Any, well-drained	○◑
Christmas berry *Heteromeles arbutifolia*	8–10	Fertile, well-drained	○◑
Cotoneaster *Cotoneaster* spp.	6–10	Any, well-drained	○◑
Currant, gooseberry *Ribes* spp.	Varies	Moist, fertile	◑
Daphne *Daphne* spp.	Varies	Moist, well-drained, deep loam	○◑
Devil's walking stick, Hercules' club *Aralia spinosa*	4–9	Any	○◑

○ Full sun ◑ Part shade ● Shade

Name	Zone	Soil	Light
Dogwood *Cornus* spp.	Varies	Rich, moist	◐
Dwarf chaparral broom *Baccharis pilularis*	8–10	Any	○
English hawthorn, Midland hawthorn *Crataegus laevigata*	4–7	Well-drained, moisture-retentive loam	○
Eucalyptus *Eucalyptus* spp.	9–10	Tolerates any; prefers rich, fertile loam	○
Euonymus *Euonymus* spp.	Varies	Any	◐
European white birch *Betula pendula*	2–7	Moist, sandy loam	◐
Fig *Ficus carica*	8–10	Moist, well-drained	○
Filbert *Corylus maxima*	6–9	Moderately fertile loam	○
Forsythia *Forsythia* spp.	5–9	Any	◐
Hankow willow, corkscrew willow *Salix matsudana*	5–8	Any	○
Heather *Calluna vulgaris*	4–7	Moist, acid	○
Heath *Erica* spp.	4–7	Moist, acid	○
Heavenly bamboo, sacred bamboo *Nandina domestica*	6–9	Clay loam	◐
Holly *Ilex* spp.	Varies	Moist, well-drained	◑
Honey flower *Melianthus major*	9–10	Poor, well-drained	◐
Iochroma *Iochroma cyanea*	9–10	Well-drained	○
Japanese flowering cherry *Prunus serrulata*	5–8	Well-drained, moisture-retentive loam	◐
Japanese kerria *Kerria japonica*	5–9	Moist, well-drained	◑●
Japanese maple *Acer palmatum*	5–8	Moist, well-drained, fertile	◑
Jasmine *Jasminum* spp.	Varies	Well-drained loam	○

○ Full sun ◐ Part shade ● Shade

Name	Zone	Soil	Light
Juniper *Juniperus* spp.	3–9	Moist, well-drained	○◑
Lantana, scrub verbena *Lantana* spp.	10	Varies	○
Lemon bottlebrush *Callistemon citrinus*	9–10	Any, except high alkaline	○◑
Lilac *Syringia* spp.	3–8	Moist, fertile	○◑
Lombardy poplar *Populus nigra* 'Italica'	3–9	Varies	○
Magnolia *Magnolia* spp.	Varies	Rich, well-drained, humusy, sandy loam	○
Mexican orange blossom *Choisya ternata*	8–10	Sandy, well-drained	○◑
Mimosa, silk tree *Albizzia julibrissin*	6–9	Rich, fertile	○
Mirror plant *Coprosma repens*	9–10	Well-drained	○
Mountain laurel *Kalmia latifolia*	4–9	Moist, peaty, humusy loam	○●
Native hops *Dodonaea viscosa*	9–10	Light, fertile, well-drained	○
Oleander *Nerium oleander*	9–10	Sandy, fertile well-drained	○◑
Oregon grape *Mahonia aquifolium*	5–8	Average	○◑
Oregon vine maple *Acer cincinatum*	5–6	Moist, fertile	◑
Pacific wax myrtle *Myrica californica*	7–10	Moist, peaty	○
Palm Many genera, many species	Varies	Average	○◑
Parryi's beargrass *Nolina parryi*	10	Sandy, well-drained	○
Pieris *Pieris japonica*	5–8	Moist, peaty, well-drained	○◑
Pine *Pinus* spp.	Varies	Light, well-drained	○◑
Podocarpus *Podocarpus* spp.	8–10	Sandy peat or loam	○◑
Pomegranate *Punica granatum*	8–10	Moist, well-drained	○◑
Red elderberry *Sambucus racemosa*	3–6	Moist, fertile, well-drained	○◑

○ Full sun ◑ Part shade ● Shade

Name	Zone	Soil	Light
Redvein enkianthus *Enkianthus campanulatus*	4–7	Moist, peaty, acid	○◑
Rhododendron* *Rhododendron* spp.	3–8	Moist, peaty, acid, well-drained	◑
Rock rose *Cistus* spp.	7–10	Friable, well-drained	○
Rosemary *Rosmarinus officinalis*	6–10	Light, well-drained	○◑
Russian olive *Elaeagnus angustifolia*	2–7	Any, well-drained	○
Salal *Gaultheria Shallon*	8–9	Sandy	◑
Sandstay, tea tree *Leptospermum* spp.	9–10	Well-drained, sandy	○
Santolina *Santolina chamaecyparissus*	6–9	Good	○
Sassafras *Sassafras albidum*	4–9	Moist, rich, well-drained	○◑
Scotch broom *Cytisus scoparius*	5–8	Any, well-drained	○
Shrubby Saint-John's-wort *Hypericum* spp.	3–8	Dry, light	◑
Silverberry *Elaeagnus commutata*	2–5	Any, well-drained	○
Smoke tree *Cotinus coggygria*	5–8	Any	○
Soapbark tree *Quillaja saponaria*	10	Sandy, well-drained	○
Spanish broom, weaver's broom *Spartium junceum*	8–10	Any	○
Spider flower *Grevillea* spp.	9–10	Sandy to medium loam	○
Spiraea *Spiraea* spp.	3–8	Any	○
Spruce *Picea* spp.	Varies	Any, well-drained	○
Strawberry tree *Arbutus unedo*	7–9	Well-drained, moist	○◑
Sugarbush *Rhus ovata*	8–10	Well-drained	○
Sweet hakea *Hakea suaveolens*	8–10	Poor	○

○ Full sun ◑ Part shade ● Shade

Name	Zone	Soil	Light
Tree peony *Paeonia suffruticosa*	4–7	Rich, fertile, well-drained	◐
Viburnum *Viburnum* spp.	Varies	Varies	Varies
Wild lilac *Ceanothus sanguineus*	6–10	Well-drained	○
Wire netting bush *Corokia cotoneaster*	6–10	Any, well-drained	○
Wisteria *Wisteria* spp.	6–8	Fertile, well-drained loam	○

* Except azalea types, which are frequently damaged in eastern states.

Plants for Hedges

Name	Zone	Soil	Light
Boxwood *Buxus* spp.	Varies	Any, well-drained	○●
Brush cherry *Syzygium paniculatum*	9–10	Varies	○
Bush germander *Teucrium fruticans*	5–9	Poor, gravelly	○
California wax myrtle *Myrica californica*	7–10	Moist, peaty	○
Carolina cherry laurel *Prunus caroliniana*	7–10	Moist, well-drained	○◐
Holly* *Ilex* spp.	Varies	Most, well-drained	◐
Jasmine *Jasminum* spp.	Varies	Well-drained, moist loam	○
Native hops *Dodonaea viscosa*	9–10	Light, fertile, well-drained	○
Oleander *Nerium oleander*	9–10	Sandy, fertile, well-drained	○◐

*Except for smooth-leafed varieties

Vines and Ground Covers

Name	Zone	Soil	Light
Algerian ivy *Hedera canariensis*	9–10	Peaty loam	○◐
American bittersweet *Celastrus scadens*	5–9	Good, fertile	○◐
Bugleweed *Ajuga repans*			○◐
Carolina yellow jasmine, jessamine *Gelsemium sempervirens*	6–9	Fertile, well-drained moist	○◐
Confederate jasmine *Trachelospermum jasminoides*	8–9	Moist, well drained	◐

○ Full sun ◐ Part shade ● Shade

Name	Zone	Soil	Light
Japanese honeysuckle *Lonicera japonica*	4–9	Moist, well-drained	○◑
Jasmine *Jasminum* spp.	Varies	Well-drained loam	○
Morning glory *Ipomoea* spp.	9–10	Rich, well-drained	○
Sweet woodruff *Galium odoratum*	4–8	Rich, well-drained	●
Vinca vine *Vinca major*	7–10	Heavy loam	◑●

Vegetables, Fruits, and Nuts

Name	Zone	Soil	Light
American persimmon *Diospyros virginiana*	4–9	Any moist, well-drained	○
Cascades mahonia *Mahonia nervosa*	5–8	Average	○◑
Cucumber *Cucumis sativus*		Rich, moist, well-drained	○
Currant, gooseberry *Ribes* spp.	Varies	Moist, fertile	○◑
Fig *Ficus carica*	8–10	Moist, well-drained	○
Filbert *Corylus maxima*	6–9	Moderately fertile loam	○
Garden onion *Allium cepa*		Any, well-drained	○
Garlic *Allium sativum*	8–10	Any, well-drained	○◑
Oregon grape *Mahonia aquifolium*	5–8	Average	○◑
Pomegranate *Punica granatum*	8–10	Moist, well-drained	○◑
Pumpkin *Cucurbita* spp.		Medium to rich, moist, well-drained	○◑
Rhubarb *Rheum x cultorum*	3–8	Light, rich	○◑
Squash *Cucurbita* spp.		Light, fertile, well-drained	○
Strawberry tree *Arbutus unedo*	7–9	Well-drained, moist	○◑

○ Full sun   ◑ Part shade   ● Shade

Compiled from numerous sources, including state Cooperative Extension Service bulletins, Master Gardener and garden club guides, and various materials published by Cornell University, Washington State University, and other institutions. When plants are listed by genus, not specific species, requirements pertain to the genus as a whole. For a particular species, more restrictive conditions may apply; consult a standard garden reference if in doubt.

Roses That Rise to the Occasion

There is hope for the die-hard rose enthusiast in deer country. Although every rose is subject to deer predation at some level, those listed below have repeatedly sustained the least damage.

	Blossom	Deterrents
Species Roses		
Rosa villosa	Mauve-pink	Tall, thorny shrub
Rosa sericea	Pink, tiny	Enormous deep red thorns
Rosa rugosa	Mauve-pink	Heavy scent; thick, dense, thorny; hedging
R. rugosa var. 'alba'	White	Heavy scent; thick, dense, thorny; hedging
R. rugosa var. 'rosea'	Deep mauve-pink	Heavy scent; thick, dense, thorny; hedging
Rosa soulieana	White	Very thorny; exceptionally tall
Rosa spinosissima	White to yellow	Very thorny, fernlike leaves
Rugosa Hybrids		
'Agnes'	Light yellow	Very thorny canes
'Belle Poitevine'	Pink	Intense scent; very thorny; very tall
'Blanc Double de Coubert'	White	Thorny; leathery leaves
'Delicata'	Mauve-pink	Very thorny; leathery leaves
'Hansa'	Red-violet	Very thorny; rugose leaves
'Roseraie de l'Hay'	Dark red purple	Thorny; leathery leaves; very tall
'Scabrosa'	Red	Thorny; rugose leaves
'Therese Bugnet'	Red-violet	Thorny; rugose leaves
'Topaz Jewel'	Yellow	Thorny; rugose leaves

Shrub Roses

'Baronne Prevost'	Pink	Very thorny; tall
'Conrad Ferdinand Meyer'	Pink	Intense fragrance; very thorny; vigorous
'Fisherman's Friend'	Crimson	Large thorns
'Harrison's Yellow'	Yellow	Very thorny; tall
'Penelope'	Coral pink	Upright, bushy; excellent hedge; tall
'Robusta'	Red	horny; vigorous growth; tall to very tall

Old Garden Roses

'Alfred de Dalmas'	Light blush pink	Very bristly, thorny; rough leaves
'Common Moss'	Pink	Very bristly, thorny; fuzzy calyxes
'Crested Moss'	Pink	Very bristly, thorny; rough leaves; tall
'Henri Martin'	Dark red	Thorny; bushy; vigorous
'General Kleber'	Medium pink	Thorny; bushy; rough leaves
'Konigin von Danemark'	Pink	Very thorny; rough leaves
'Louis Gimard'	Mauve-pink	Very thorny; pine-scented, mossy buds
'Madame de la Roche-Lambert'	Pink	Very thorny, arching canes; rough leaves
'Maiden's Blush'	Light blush pink	Very fragrant; bristly; thorny; tall
'Striped Moss'	Red-and-white striped	Very thorny; rough leaves; mossy
'William Lobb'	Deep mauve	Bristly, thorny; mossy; heavily scented
'York & Lancaster'	Pink and white	Very bristly, thorny; rough leaves

Plants That (Usually) Repel Deer

It gets even better: Some plants actually deter deer. They don't even like to get near them. Most notable are some highly fragrant plants. Heavy scent masks other odors, effectively jamming the deer's predator-alert sensors and making them uneasy. No one knows for sure why some deer are more sensitive to odiferous plants than others, though the degree of sensitivity probably depends on many variables in the deer's life. There is no guarantee as to how individual deer will react, but based on research and the experience of thousands of gardeners, the following plants appear to be deer bane:

Common	Botanic	Zone	Soil	Light
Catmint, catnip	*Nepeta* spp.	3–8	Well-drained	Sun
Chives, garlic, onions	*Allium* spp.	5–10	Loose	Sun
Honeybush	*Melianthus major*	8–10	Acid	Shade
Lavender	*Lavendula* spp.	5–9	Well-drained	Sun
Sage	*Salvia* spp.	4–8	Well-drained	Sun
Society garlic	*Tulbaghia violacea*	8–10	Fertile	Sun
Spearmint	*Mentha* spp.	4–9	Any	Any
Thyme	*Thymus* spp.	4–10	Well-drained	Any
Yarrow	*Achillea* spp.	3–10	Any	Any

TESTING FOR PALATABILITY

It figures. You scoured the lists and the plants you're concerned about aren't even mentioned. Don't fret; there are ways to determine if a new plant will be considered bait or bane by neighborhood deer. For example, place a sample in a pot and leave it where deer are known to feed. For small plants this could be an entire potted specimen, for larger plants, a cutting or branch. If the deer leave it alone, it should be safe to plant. If they devour it, try something else. However, deer might avoid a new plant in a strange container only because, ever wary of the unfamiliar, they are avoiding the *container*. Leave the empty container in their area for a few days before attempting to test any new plants.

When considering new plants for the garden, compare them with related plants. Often this will provide a clue as to whether or not they're likely to wind up as deer fodder. Pay particular attention to wild plants in your area that deer leave alone. For instance, deer don't eat mayweed (*Anthemis cotula*) and will also leave such relatives as golden marguerite (*Anthemis tinctoria*) alone. The buttercup (*Ranunculus* spp., of the Ranunculaceae family) is toxic to deer and therefore avoided, as are such closely related plants as delphiniums (also of the Ranunculaceae) and peonies (formerly classified as Ranunculaceae, now listed as Paeoniaceae). On the other hand, most roses (family Rosaceae) are like deer candy, and related plants, such as apples, cherries, and raspberries, all suffer the same fate when deer venture by.

TRICKS OF THE TRADE

When you design a garden to avoid deer damage, the most important considerations — the purpose of your garden and the overall look you desire — don't change. But you can accomplish

> Do you long for spring-flowering bulbs? Then ditch the tulips and deploy daffodils.

most goals more than one way. Many of your favorite plants that deer greedily scarf down have relatively deer proof counterparts that can fulfill the same function. Do you long for spring-flowering bulbs? Then ditch the tulips and deploy daffodils. Need a shady spot in the summer yard? Fig, birch, horse chestnut, and mature common lilac trees will fill the bill, not fill a deer's stomach. Need a hedge for privacy? Forget about such deer delicacies as hemlock and yew, and concentrate on junipers or rugosa roses.

Once you compile a list of suitable substitutes, factor in any plants you really can't live without. Careful design (and perhaps some of the deterrents listed in the next chapter) should allow you to enjoy deer-tempting favorites with little or no damage. The purpose of deer-o-scape design is to make it appear to the deer that you grow only fuzzy, stinky, yucky-tasting stuff and that they may as well seek supper elsewhere. Remember, being the creatures of habit that they are, once deer determine that your yard is absolutely tasteless, you'll have less trouble with returning foragers.

Try these deer-o-scaping tricks:

SUBSTITUTE THE UNSAVORY. As mentioned, for nearly every plant that deer pilfer, there's bound to be at least one substitute that deer detest. Though hybrid tea roses are favored fare, an intense scent, thorny canes, leathery leaves, and a propensity to sprawl into impenetrable barriers combine to make many rugosa hybrids nearly deer proof. Categorize the plants in your garden by function, form, color, and so forth, then shop the lists of plants deer avoid for some suitable alternatives.

CREATE UNINVITING ENTRYWAYS. Whether through the driveway, an open field, or an alley, chances are deer enter your property through a routine route. Make sure deer find the entryway to your garden unattractive. Concentrate deer-repelling plants here.

FOUL THE FRINGES. Keep your "edges" equally unattractive. Line *your* territory with unpalatable and repellent plants and chances are the deer will keep to *their* territory and pass your no-longer-tempting yard by.

MIX CONFUSING COMBINATIONS. "I was sure there were daylilies in there somewhere," Bambi complains to Faline, "but all I could smell was garlic." The moral: Deer won't eat what they can't detect, no matter how much a preferred food it is. Surrounding and interplanting susceptible plants with unpalatable or repellent plants makes them much harder for deer to find, and — guilt by association — much less attractive if they are detected.

DEPLOY DECEPTIVE DEFENSES. Smaller plants can be camouflaged by deterrent companions. Larger plants, such as young trees and shrubs, can be defended by completely surrounding them with unappetizing companions.

PROVIDE NO VIEW. Any portions of yard obscured from sight are much less likely to encourage deer to enter than those with a clear view. Create a deer barrier from a garden border using solid hedges grown from rugosa roses or junipers, or from trellises swathed in morning glory. Deer won't venture past anything they can't see through or over.

ELIMINATE UNNECESSARY COVER. Tall grass, brushy borders, and areas of your property left to grow wild all encourage deer to bed down. Keep grass and underbrush trimmed and tidy near the garden to discourage loitering.

BE TIDY. It's never wise to leave fruit rotting on the vine or tree. Few things entice deer like ripe apples and pears. So be a tidy gardener. Keep fruit picked up (this also reduces the threat of other pests, including yellow jackets) and remove or till under the remains of deer-favored crops, such as corn and peas, as soon as harvest is finished.

PROVIDE NO LANDING SITE. Deer won't attempt to leap into your yard if it appears they have no landing site. This depends more on the lay of your land than other deer proofing techniques, but incorporating terraces and multiple levels around the perimeter of your plot may help to discourage deer from alighting on your lawn.

MAKE THEM A BETTER OFFER. "Why brave the garden close to the house when they planted the good stuff all the way out here?" the deer may wonder as they contentedly munch soybeans on the outskirts of your property. Commercial growers successfully use lure crops, which may help detour deer from the plants you want to protect. Some gardeners distract deer with other food, such as dried corn, alfalfa hay, apples, or bread. A plot of corn left standing unhusked in the fall or an alfalfa, buckwheat, clover, or rye grass patch should tempt deer away from other plants.

ADOPT XERISCAPE TECHNIQUES. Xeriscaping evolved as a gardening style tailored to the needs of gardens under chronic drought conditions. The tenets are simple: Do more with less, and conserve water — both of which also make sense in the deer-plagued garden. Xeriscaped gardens have a distinctive look. No endlessly rolling stretches of green on green, these gardens are designed to look natural, yet defined. Gravel pathways of contrasting colored rock serve as borders and punctuation lines. Attractive mulches (most of which deer don't eat) conserve water and draw the eye. Drought-tolerant plants in carefully planned positions give the appearance of more greenery than there actually is. Moreover, many classic Xeriscaping plants are avoided by deer regardless of how much water the plants receive and, when stressed by drought, are tough and taste bad.

TRY TASTELESS LAWN ORNAMENTS. Just as Xeriscaping takes the focus off many green growing things and redirects it toward specifically designed points of interest, so too can other gardening styles. You don't necessarily need a full flock of flaming flamingos to replace the visual appeal normally supplied by greenery. Garden seats, sundials, trellises, sculpture, and fountains make wonderful focal points in the landscape. Consider removing any deer-luring plants and replacing them with nonedible points of interest.

GARDEN DESIGNS THAT DISCOURAGE DEER

A deer-o-scaped yard need know few limitations. Follow these four steps to create your deer-resistant garden:

1. Identify and accept the things you can't change, such as temperature extremes, overall soil type, and yearly rainfall.

2. Define your space. Decide where play, parking, and garden areas belong.

3. Look up, look down. Incorporate vertical plants and ground cover for variety.

4. Indulge your personal taste. Choose the colors, textures, and scents *you* prefer.

Each step will help you progressively narrow down the choices on the deer-resistant plant list. Use the remaining options as the building blocks of your deer-o-scaped yard. Other, nonresistant favorites can be interplanted with relative safety, especially if you wait until the deer become accustomed to your unappetizing choices.

The following pages offer five sample garden designs based on deer-resistant plants and deer-o-scaping techniques:

- Cold-tolerant garden. For areas that experience severe winter chill, choose the most cold-tolerant plants from the deer-resistant plant list.

- Sunny garden with ample moisture. These are the easiest gardening conditions and present you with the most options. If this describes your garden, be grateful and indulge!

- Dry, sunny garden. This design emphasizes drought-tolerant plants but still offers a luxurious yard.

- Dry, shady garden. Dry shade ranks among the most challenging of gardening conditions, but the number of deer-resistant options may surprise you.

- Boggy, shady garden. You can create a lush yard and garden by choosing from the many plants that *prefer* damp shade.

Of course, many yards don't fit neatly into just one of these categories, and you may therefore need to combine parts of two or three of these sample designs. Substitute and experiment to personalize your own outdoor living space.

Cold-Tolerant Garden

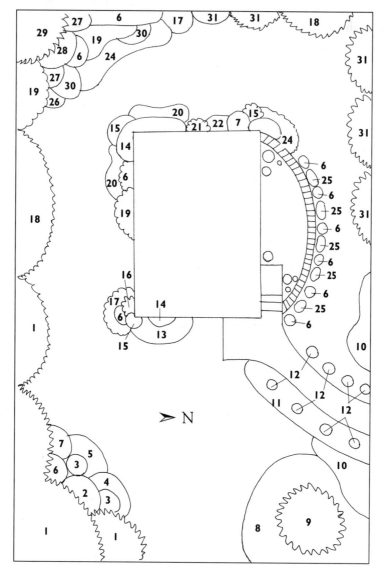

> N

1 Juniper	12 Korean boxwood	23 Lady's mantle
2 Saint-John's-wort	13 Forget-me-nots	24 Dead nettle
3 Yarrow	14 Peony	25 Chives
4 Poppies	15 Borage	26 Lupine
5 Golden marguerite	16 Salvia	27 Foxglove
6 Iris	17 Ageratum	28 Larkspur
7 Columbine	18 Holly	29 English hawthorn
8 Snowflake	19 Cranesbill geranium	30 Lamb's ears
9 Spruce	20 Rose campion	31 Creeping juniper
10 Daffodil	21 Catmint	
11 Thyme	22 Bleeding heart	

Cold-Tolerant Garden

Deer country is often cold country, a fact that pits the gardener against two adversaries — deer and harsh winter temperatures. Deer in cold climes often eat anything, even blatantly poisonous plants, if they are starving, and much of the deer damage done to ornamentals consists of bark stripped and twigs and buds consumed during the cruelest part of winter.

Bordered by the street on the north side, a brick-walled courtyard bars entry to deer from the front. Pots, furniture, and other items placed inside the courtyard make for an uncertain landing, and deer generally won't chance vaulting the wall. A surrounding border of iris and chives offers nothing appetizing for the deer. The driveway, too, is bordered by unappealing plants, from thyme, which releases its deer-deterring scent whenever it gets stepped on, to bitter-tasting daffodils, to unpalatable boxwood shrubs. A huge Colorado blue spruce in the northeast corner can take any winter nature dishes out and is rarely disturbed by deer. Underplanting with a naturalizing flurry of mildly toxic snowflake adds to the woodland character of the corner.

The area south of the spruce remains open, offering no cover for deer. However, lest any passing deer choose to enter, toxic peonies, fuzzy forget-me-nots, and fuzzier borage are among the first plantings it would find. A bed at the far southeast corner of the yard features junipers and various distasteful perennials. Nearby, two shrubs, holly and pungent juniper, add privacy to the yard.

The southwest corner includes prickly English hawthorn, which affords a privacy screen, and a foul fringe that includes dead nettle; fuzzy lamb's ears; and toxic foxglove, larkspur, and lupine. Add to that the repellent odor of catmint and unappealing taste and texture of bleeding heart, lady's mantle, columbine, and peony, and deer will quickly forsake any forays.

The western edge of the yard is partially obscured from view by shrubbery, and tangles of mat-forming aromatic juniper create uncertain footing along the northwest corner.

Sunny Garden with Ample Moisture

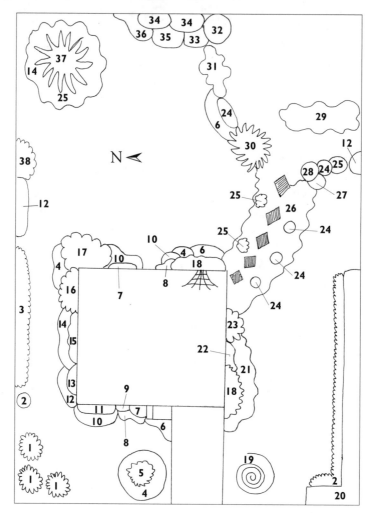

1 Podocarpus (zones 8–10) or euonymus (colder zones)
2 Boxwood
3 Barberry
4 Rose campion
5 Magnolia
6 Ageratum
7 Cape plumbago
8 Salvia
9 Catnip
10 Dusty miller
11 Rosemary
12 Iris
13 Foxglove
14 Forget-me-nots
15 Ferns
16 Spiraea
17 Butterfly bush
18 Fairy rose
19 Corkscrew willow
20 Japanese wisteria trained on an arbor
21 Cranesbill geranium
22 Larkspur
23 Borage
24 Chives
25 Ornamental allium
26 Thyme
27 Oregano
28 Parsley
29 Squash
30 Sage
31 Rhubarb
32 Mint
33 Snapdragon
34 Japanese rose
35 Zinnia
36 Lemon marigold
37 Weeping cherry
38 Lily of the Nile

Sunny Garden with Ample Moisture

Lots of sun, plenty of water — these are the conditions that turn a gardener's thumbs green, and it's all the more distressing when deer take down the fruits of your labor.

This sample garden starts with a privacy screen of podocarpus. An attractive, versatile small tree, podocarpus is rarely damaged by deer. Immediately within the screen, a foundation planting of such unscrumptious fare as forget-me-nots, ferns, foxglove, and sticky-stemmed rose campion serves as an uninviting entryway. A screen of barberry along the northern edge of the property forms a barrier hedge, while neither lily of the Nile nor iris tempts hungry deer. A weeping cherry, underplanted with forget-me-nots and spires of flowering allium, provides a focal point for the open backyard.

A large portion of this yard is dedicated to a vegetable and herb garden. To keep deer away, the garden has been disguised with a scented flower border. Such deer bane as marigolds, snapdragons, and zinnias frame taller, view-obscuring plants, such as Japanese rose. Aromatic sage, chives, and mint reinforce a deer's negative impression, and large rhubarb leaves further block the view. The other side of the garden is bordered by equally unappealing alliums, iris, parsley, and oregano.

For privacy without the protective cover that often lures deer, try a formally trained wisteria arbor. The front of the trellising system is edged in boxwood. The walkway between the garden and house features thyme and other scented plants.

Foundation plantings of fairy rose, geranium, dusty miller, and rose campion are color coordinated. Deer may nibble a fairy rose now and then, but the plant's prickly nature slows them down somewhat and its aggressive growth outpaces their damage. Other foundation plants, such as salvia and cape plumbago, are attractive to humans, not deer.

The short driveway is accentuated by specimen trees that deer ignore. Underplanting with vinca or rose campion further frustrates any meandering deer. Bitter-tasting ageratum, salvia, and aromatic herbs stop deer at the front yard and offer no invitation to explore further.

Dry, Sunny Garden

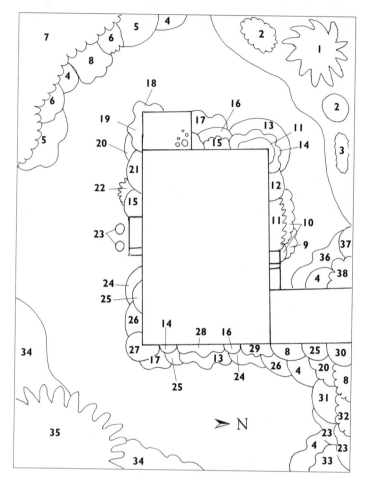

1 Drooping she oak	14 Lavender	27 Carolina cherry laurel
2 Spider flower	15 Rock rose	28 Red valerian
3 Juniper	16 Aloe	29 Ice plant
4 Artemisia	17 Rosemary	30 Redhot poker
5 Blue fescue	18 Zinnia	31 Gloriosa daisy
6 Fennel	19 Pot marigold	32 Everlasting
7 Bush germander	20 Tansy	33 Yucca
8 Santolina	21 Oregon grape	34 Sweet hakea
9 Aster	22 Yarrow	35 Pine
10 Dusty miller	23 Sage	36 Veronica
11 Iris	24 Hen-and-chickens	37 Poppy
12 Epimedium	25 Russian sage	38 Pride of Madeira
13 Verbena	26 Purple coneflower	

Dry, Sunny Garden

Gardeners have discovered that a dry, sun-drenched yard is really just an oasis waiting to happen. The trick is to master the conversion without squandering precious moisture and without inviting in a whole herd of deer.

The northwest corner of the yard is dominated by a drooping she oak, bounded on either side by spider flower and mulched in decorative gravel. The trees require little water and, to the deer, they have about the same consistency as the gravel. The grouping affords little cover, creating an uninviting entryway.

Full and varied borders drape both sides of the driveway. On one side pride of Madeira serves as a focal point, while the fragrance of artemisia spreads out to discourage deer. The opposite side sports stately redhot pokers surrounded by crowds of heavily scented sage, tansy, santolina, and artemisia. A tall, tough, tasteless yucca guards the northeast corner.

Along the east side of the house, succulents, such as ice plant and hen-and-chickens, vie with red valerian (Jupiter's beard) and purple coneflower for attention. Lavender and rosemary reinforce the distracting scents in the air. An open area beyond the scented borders leads, on the southeast, to a privacy screen of thorny sweet hakea, backed by a mature pine tree. Too high for deer to clear, these are in no danger of deer damage.

The foundation plants at the rear of the house are scaled down to allow for the narrow backyard while still providing color and interest. Sage offers both bright flowers and a perfume that deer detest. The other plantings are no more tempting, while the open backyard provides no cover.

To the southwest, a low hedge of bush germander, underplanted with thickly scented shrubs and ornamental grasses, conceals the patio area. This layout offers no visible landing site should deer consider leaping. A lush border fans out from the edges of the patio, combining bright blooms with still more deer-deterring scents. This border leads right up to the front door, greeting any nondeer visitor with cheerful blooms and rich foliage. With nowhere to hide and so much fragrance in the air, this is not a yard where deer will linger.

Dry, Shady Garden

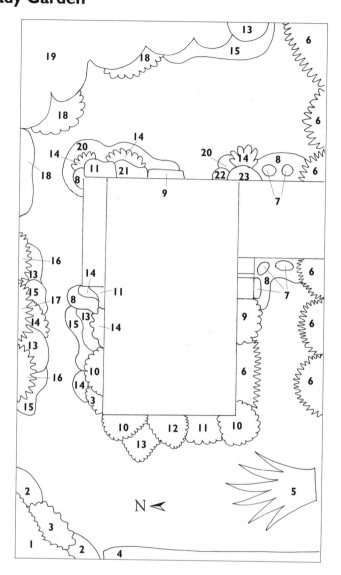

1 Saint-John's-wort
2 Oregon grape
3 Lady's mantle
4 Holly
5 Pampas grass
6 Juniper
7 Heath
8 Thyme
9 Jasmine

10 Butcher's broom
11 Epimedium
12 Salal
13 Artemisia
14 Lamb's ears
15 Dead nettle
16 Stinking iris
17 Redhot poker
18 Winter currant

19 Bottlebrush
20 Vinca
21 Australian fuchsia
   (Zone 8) or jasmine
   (colder zones)
22 Borage
23 Wild bleeding heart

Dry, Shady Garden

Turning a dry, dark garden into a gardener's dream may seem like an impossible nightmare, but it can be done. Many deer-resistant plants will thrive here. Some may need supplemental watering, but good organization will allow you to incorporate them. Group together plants that require the least water, positioning them near the edge of the yard, if possible.

The northwest corner of this garden offers a low screen of deer-resistant shrubbery, including Saint-John's-wort and Oregon grape. The dense and prickly texture of these shrubs creates a nearly impenetrable corner, without a clear landing site. A nearby bed features highly aromatic plants (stinking iris, artemisia) that deer dislike. Farther down the property line, a hedge of closely planted bottlebrush trees, fronted with a flowering currant (*Ribes sanguineum*), creates a screen that obscures the view into the yard. An artemisia stands sentry at the southeast end.

Low-growing junipers line the front walk, which lends landscape interest and offends the deer's sense of smell. Their fragrance carries throughout much of the yard. The driveway is planted on either side with heath and thyme, which deer find equally uninviting.

Foundation plantings are surprisingly varied, given the limitations of the growing conditions. Wild bleeding heart and borage contribute a lush bit of contrasting greenery, while trellised jasmine scents the air. Planted at the foot of the jasmine, a carpet of distasteful vinca spreads out to embrace much of the patio foliage. Epimedium provides a hostalike green backdrop for other plants. Near the patio the heavy scents of additional plantings of thyme and artemisia camouflage any other plants that you choose to grow there.

To the west, a holly hedge provides a wall of seclusion. The deer can't see through it, let alone walk through it. At the south end of the hedge is a tough, tasteless, splendid patch of pampas grass. Coming around the west side of the house, juniper and butcher's broom lead to an assortment of plants that deer find foul-tasting, smelly, or fuzzy.

Boggy, Shady Garden

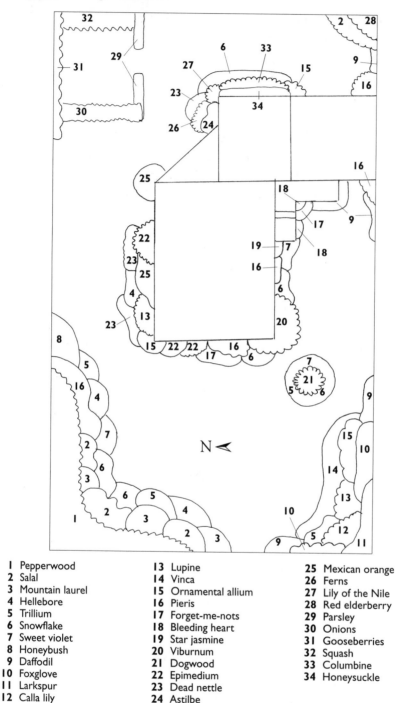

1 Pepperwood	13 Lupine	25 Mexican orange
2 Salal	14 Vinca	26 Ferns
3 Mountain laurel	15 Ornamental allium	27 Lily of the Nile
4 Hellebore	16 Pieris	28 Red elderberry
5 Trillium	17 Forget-me-nots	29 Parsley
6 Snowflake	18 Bleeding heart	30 Onions
7 Sweet violet	19 Star jasmine	31 Gooseberries
8 Honeybush	20 Viburnum	32 Squash
9 Daffodil	21 Dogwood	33 Columbine
10 Foxglove	22 Epimedium	34 Honeysuckle
11 Larkspur	23 Dead nettle	
12 Calla lily	24 Astilbe	

Boggy, Shady Garden

If your home is settled in swampy territory, you may find it a haven for neighborhood deer. They especially like the dense cover and tender foliage such conditions produce. Remember that many plants that deer eat when the menu is limited are often ignored when there are tastier treats available. Capitalize on the surrounding environment; if there is sufficient forage for deer outside your yard, be bold and plant a few of your favorites along with some of the plants in this sample garden.

The northwest corner offers a view-obscuring screen of deer-resistant plants, anchored by pepperwood and layered in different heights. All of the plants in the screen are unpalatable to deer but attractive to us. The edge of the border, a possible entryway for deer, is made uninviting by a fragrant honeybush, which deer find repugnant. A row of gooseberries shields the northernmost border of a potential garden plot from the view of passing deer, while unappealing squash and parsley line other borders. In addition, onions protect the most vulnerable side of the area.

The patio is framed in ferns and dramatic lily of the Nile, both of which deer find tasteless. Mexican orange and sweet violets swath the area in fragrance. For privacy, the area next to the driveway is planted in attractive pieris, the texture of which deer dislike. In addition, deer avoid the oniony smell of the nearby alliums. With nothing good to eat within sight or scent of the open driveway, deer pass it by. At the southeast corner of the yard, red elderberry defeats deer not only by being toxic, but also by aggressive growth that outpaces any deer damage.

The foundation plantings are lush with greenery, flowers, and fragrance from plants that deer find distasteful. A favorite for thick, green growth, epimedium, offers the same verdant backdrop as hostas while not attracting dining deer. A flowering dogwood is underplanted with fragrant and toxic plants, while a viburnum; onion-scented alliums; and toxic foxglove, lupine, and larkspur foul the fringes of the side yard.

Deer Deterrents

Not since Eden has a gardener been content to sit idly by and watch the deer of the field consume his bounty. Gardeners work hard for the rewards the deer so nonchalantly pillage.

If you've applied the deer-o-scaping principles and suggestions discussed in Chapter 4, you should be on your way to curbing your deer problem. Unfortunately, even strict adherence to the deer-o-scaping guidelines won't guarantee success, and deer-o-scaping is only of limited value to those of you with well-established plantings that you are loath to uproot. So, what next?

If deer-o-scaping represents benign intervention, we still need to consider more aggressive measures — active deterrents, including home remedies, chemical agents, and other commercial products, plus, in the next chapter, fences. First, however, you need to be clear about what you hope to accomplish.

DEFINING YOUR OBJECTIVE

Simply put, what is your objective? To eliminate the deer or to minimize the damage they cause? Think of damage in terms of such factors as economic and aesthetic loss — for example, how long browsed ornamentals take to recover — and your level of tolerance. Damage that one gardener may consider absolutely unbearable another doesn't even notice.

The accompanying chart offers an overview of how assessing population conditions and relative damage can help you determine what management techniques to adopt. If the deer population is low and damage slight — in other words, if the natural habitat adequately supports the deer concentration, resulting in low deer pressure — you can reasonably expect to alleviate deer damage to your garden altogether, probably using deer-o-scaping and some simple deterrents. (Note, however, that even if deer *population* is relatively low, *pressure* on your plot of land may still be high, especially if the surrounding landscape offers lean pickings.) If population is high and damage excessive (high deer pressure), nothing

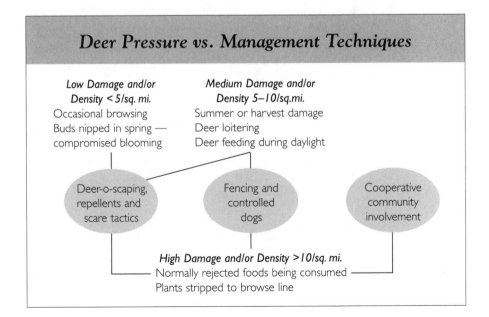

Deer Pressure vs. Management Techniques

Low Damage and/or Density < 5/sq. mi.
Occasional browsing
Buds nipped in spring —
compromised blooming

Medium Damage and/or Density 5–10/sq.mi.
Summer or harvest damage
Deer loitering
Deer feeding during daylight

Deer-o-scaping, repellents and scare tactics

Fencing and controlled dogs

Cooperative community involvement

High Damage and/or Density > 10/sq. mi.
Normally rejected foods being consumed
Plants stripped to browse line

short of elaborate fencing and community control efforts (see Chapter 7) may suffice. Even then, you may have to consider a substantial reduction in deer damage as an absolute success.

In sum, first assess the severity of the problem, then define your goal, and, last, choose your tactics.

WHY DETERRENTS DO OR DON'T WORK

A few points that have already been stated bear repeating because they essentially determine why deer deterrents do or don't work:

◆ A deer's first priority is not to get eaten. Deterrents that take advantage of predator avoidance behavior have a great record of success.

◆ Deer in wild country react differently from deer that have adjusted to the presence of humans. Suburban gardeners have to be a tad more resourceful than their country cousins.

◆ Deer are creatures of habit. Their previous experience with any given food or deterrent dictates their future response to the same or similar circumstances. *Preventing deer damage before it starts is easier than interrupting an established pattern.*

◆ Deer are, however, adaptable. No matter how effective a deterrent may be when you first employ it, chances are that unless it jumps up and comes after them, the deer will invariably get wise to the fact that it can't eat them. And once they adapt to your garden, they adopt it.

The most frustrating thing about dealing with deer damage is that deterrents that work fabulously in one setting may not help at all in another, or even in the same setting at another time. Differences in how deer react to deterrents occur from species to species, region to region, individual to individual, season to season, and for no apparent reason. Whitetails tend to adapt to human activities more quickly than deer that haven't lived in our midst as long, but all deer are maddeningly adept at adapting to our efforts to keep them at bay.

Five Sensible Approaches

The individual variability of deer and their enviable adaptability would be problem enough, but you also have to contend with their superior physical senses. Given all this, it may seem as though they have the advantage against gardeners merely trying to protect their plants. Well, maybe they do. But we can use our superior *reasoning* ability to exploit those superior senses and thereby get the results we want. We *can* succeed.

The deer's five physical senses give us five different ways to assault their sense of security and send them scampering back to the woods (or at least over to the neighbor's yard). Like all wild animals, deer are neophobic (afraid of anything new). The strange and the unpredictable spell trouble to a prey species. So the trick is not to give them a chance to adapt. Thus, the most important advice in any deer deterrent program: Plan on using *several* deterrent tactics, and rotating and alternating them throughout the course of the season, *before* the deer get used to them. That way, mysterious and frightening deterrents become all the more mysterious and frightening.

Assaulting all five senses also gives you some choices as to what you can tolerate in your yard, for some of the things suggested to repel deer are equally effective on gardeners. Always weigh the severity of the deer damage against the inconvenience, unsightliness, and/or cost of the deterrents.

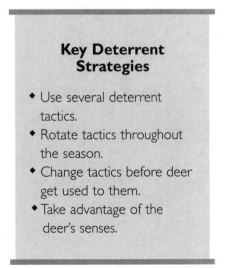

Key Deterrent Strategies

- Use several deterrent tactics.
- Rotate tactics throughout the season.
- Change tactics before deer get used to them.
- Take advantage of the deer's senses.

Battle Preparations

Since deer migrate or yard up in the winter and become more active again in the spring, early spring is the optimum time to set up your chosen deer deterrents. If deer are a problem in the area, or have been a problem in the near past, don't delay taking action. Wait-and-see won't work. Preventing potential deer damage has a higher success rate than altering existing habits. Start a prevention program *before* you see deer damage.

For most types of garden pests, the prevailing wisdom is to start with the least drastic solution and advance to harsher treatments if the first wave doesn't do the trick. The problem with this concept when it comes to deer is that they will progressively learn that every tactic you try is basically harmless, just another odd piece of landscaping. And meanwhile they will be indulging themselves at your expense. The first wave has to count.

From fouling their sense of smell to surprising their sense of touch, the tactics discussed in the rest of this chapter have all been used successfully by gardeners throughout the United States and Canada. Some of these strategies may sound a little extreme; most are genuinely harmless. However, be cautious. Avoid repellents that may harm plants. If in doubt, test the deterrent on a small portion of a plant before making an all-out application. Most importantly, never plant, place, or position anything in your garden that might be poisonous or harmful to pets, people, or even wildlife. This goes equally for home remedies or repellent plants, such as the poisonous castor oil bean, as it does for commercial preparations and chemicals. The aim of the deer-proof garden is to prevent or minimize deer damage, not to harm wildlife or innocent bystanders.

FOUL SMELLS

We know that deer have a very sensitive sense of smell and rely heavily on it. So we can be real stinkers (to the deer) when we need to be. There are two strategies to deter deer through scent: jamming their sensors, so to speak, and setting off a red alert. Both approaches call for area repellents — that is, disseminated repellents that carry lingering odors. How big an area is protected depends on the repellent and how you use it.

There are two strategies to deter deer through scent:
- ◆ Jamming their sensors
- ◆ Setting off a red alert

Scent deterrents that "jam the deer's sensors" are so strongly scented that deer in their vicinity have trouble scenting through them. These scents don't necessarily have to be offensive to humans, just intense. Not being able to scent the wind for danger is an uncomfortable situation for deer, and they can't tolerate it for long.

"Red alert" deterrents offer a more direct approach and are more effective, when used properly, than masking scents. These are predator scents that, rather than block the whispers of other scents on the wind, scream, *"Run for your life!"*

Bear in mind that garden conditions may require frequent applications to keep repellent scents fresh and effective. Most need reapplication after a heavy rain, though humid conditions actually enhance odors. Don't forget that deer feed from ground level to as high as six feet (that's six feet above the *snow line* in winter) and that repellents must be applied within that range. Many hold their repellent qualities longer if protected in containers. Some suggestions for homemade containers are included with the specific repellents discussed below, but savvy garden suppliers have designer containers available.

Early-spring applications protect the garden as new growth begins to emerge. Reapplications keep the level of protection up throughout the growing season. And if applied in late fall, before temperatures dip below freezing, repellents protect evergreens and other vulnerable plants from winter browsing.

Finally, remember that deer get used to new odors and may decide, in time, that any given odor repellent is not much of a threat. Be sure to keep them guessing by changing the location and type of repellent from time to time.

Soap

Scented soaps repel deer. Just who discovered this is uncertain, but leaving bars of soap about the garden scares deer away. Bar soaps and their chemical counterparts, ammonium soaps of higher fatty acids, are both fairly effective in repelling deer.

TO USE: Drill a small hole through each soap bar, tie with string, and hang about the yard or in tree or shrub branches. Leave the wrappers on to prevent soap from washing away. Alternatively, place soap in cheesecloth bags or old nylon stockings and tie the sudsy little sachets around the garden.

Positioning of the soap is important to prevent deer from browsing between the bars. Yes, scientific tests have actually been conducted to determine just how close deer can stand to feed next to soap, and the consensus is about three feet. That comes to approximately 450 bars to the acre. For a large garden, that's a lot of soap. Many home gardeners find the best use of soap is hanging it in fruit or ornamental trees whose branches may fall victim to deer damage.

Which brand of soap you choose doesn't appear to be critical. Some people insist that heavily scented deodorant soaps, such as Irish Spring, are most effective. You might, however, want to avoid soaps containing edible oils as a main ingredient, since at least one report recounted deer actually eating the coconut oil soap Tone.

PROS AND CONS: Hanging soap in the garden is fairly effective in preventing deer from browsing within three feet of the bar. It's inexpensive (on a per-tree basis), safe, and easy to

Leaving the wrappers on, hang bars of soap throughout the garden or on individual trees and shrubs.

install, and the bars need not be replaced until they have nearly been washed away by rain or sprinkler water.

One problem, however, is that the same soap fats that repel deer can attract rodents. As soap washes down the branches and trunks of trees and shrubs, it lures rodents to chew on the bark. To prevent rodent damage, combine the use of soaps with a rodent repellent. Hot pepper mixes (see "Bad Tastes", page 99) will repel both the big browsers and the little nibblers.

RELATED COMMERCIAL PRODUCTS: Soap-based commercial preparations include Hinder. Unlike many other such deterrents, Hinder is approved by the United States Department of Agriculture to be applied directly to plants that are to be eaten. Although regarded as almost twice as effective as hanging bars of soap, it does not weather well and for best results should be applied with an antidesiccant, such as Wilt-Pruf or Vapor Gard.

Hair

Human hair is saturated with our scent and as such proves an effective deterrent against wild deer. More-urbanized deer, however, are far too sophisticated to be put off by this, and using human hair as a repellent is generally a wasted effort. If you want to give it a try, pay your local hairdresser a visit wtih empty bags in hand and offer to sweep up. Hair from predators, when available, works well. No need to shave a lion: Dog groomers sweep up and discard buckets of predator hair.

TO USE: Stuff handfuls of hair or fur into cheesecloth bags or sections of old nylons and tie closed. Place the hair about the garden and/or hang from trees and shrubs. As with soap bars, the hair bags should be placed no more than three feet apart.

PROS AND CONS: The pros are that hair is free, easy to come by, and often works to deter deer. The cons are that some deer will ignore the smell and that even if the hair scent does work, it must be restocked every few weeks, as it gradually loses its odor.

Repellent Plants

Interplanting repellent plants with more-vulnerable species is a valuable technique in the art of deer-o-scaping. Heavily scented herbs, such as artemisia, lavender, Russian sage, tansy, and yarrow, as well as culinary herbs, including thyme, tarragon, oregano, dill, and chives, often prove intolerable to deer. Planting chives, onions, garlic, and any related members of the onion (*Allium*) genus near prize posies helps to keep the latter from becoming deer snacks. Oddly, plants toxic to deer, such as foxglove, don't appear to have repellent properties, as deer frequently feed among them.

TO USE: Refer to Chapter Four, "Deer-o-Scaping."

PROS AND CONS: Though strategic plantings call for a good deal of thoughtful planning, they can succeed in discouraging deer traffic in areas of low-to-moderate deer pressure. Specific herbs and deterrent plants are readily available through mail-order outlets, if not closer to home.

Garlic and Rotten Eggs

The sulfur compounds contained in garlic and fermented egg solids are highly repellent to deer and other garden pests. Deterrents made from these ingredients are among the most effective scent repellents available.

TO USE: Concoct your own homemade version by processing 1 egg per cup of water in a blender or with a hand mixer. Leave the slurry to ferment for several days before applying to plants. Bits of egg may remain suspended in the mixture, which can clog sprayer nozzles, so the best way to apply the solution is to pour or sprinkle it over the foliage of vulnerable plants. Add a clove of garlic to the mix and a dash of chili pepper or Tabasco sauce for extra punch, to double its effectiveness.

Another option: garlic socks. Stuff old socks or stockings with crushed or bruised cloves of garlic and hang in shrubs or trees.

PROS AND CONS: Fermented egg solids and strong garlic scents rank among the most repellent odors out there, short of hot lion's breath. These aromas are so pungent that *you* may not be able to stand the smell of the mixture as you prepare or apply it. Fortunately, after the egg mixture dries on the plants and surrounding soil, people find the aroma much less noticeable, but the deer's superior sense of smell will still detect it.

RELATED COMMER-CIAL PRODUCTS: The proliferation of commercial deer repellents based on the sulfur compounds found in garlic or eggs offers substantial evidence

> ### *Eau de Rotten Eggs*
>
> 2 eggs
> 2 cups water
> 1 to 4 cloves garlic
> 2 tablespoons Tabasco (optional)
>
> *At high speed in blender, puree garlic in water. Add other ingredients and process mixture thoroughly. Allow it to rest, covered, for several days prior to application.*

that these scents effectively deter deer. Examples include Deer Away (also sold as Big Game Repellent, or B.G.R.), Deer Off, and N.I.M.B.Y. Deer Away is registered for use on fruit trees, nurseries, ornamentals, and conifer seedlings, but not approved for food crops. Highly recommended, it maintains its effectiveness for up to forty days with a single application, regardless of rainfall. Deer Off also clings after a rain and is environmentally friendly.

The big advantage to commercial products is that you don't have to mix them up yourself. Also, they can be sprayed, making them easier to use and ensuring more even application to foliage than sprinkling the homemade brew. Uniform application is less of a concern, however, with scent repellents than with taste, or contact, deterrents. Cost may be a drawback, and most cannot be used on food crops.

Fabric Softener Strips

One of the cheapest and easiest repellents you can try is fabric softener strips — the kind you use in your dryer. The stronger the fragrance, the better.

TO USE: Tie or hang fabric softener strips in or near susceptible plants. Hang them at intervals of three feet (as recommended for soap or hair).

PROS AND CONS: "Springtime fresh" or floral scents blend into the garden better than the smell of rotten eggs, and fabric softener strips are easy enough to install. However, the strips quickly become waterlogged after a rain and must be replaced. Even so, they remain relatively inexpensive and are worth a try.

Mothballs

Also known as naphthalene, mothballs or flakes have long been used as area repellents. Gardeners report success in deterring deer, squirrels, and skunks, among other creatures, with the noxious fumes.

TO USE: Put several mothballs or a handful of flakes into cheesecloth or old nylon bags and place about the garden. Sprinkling loose balls or flakes also provides good repelling properties but increases the potential for exposure to unintended victims, such as wild birds, cats, and other pets.

PROS AND CONS: Though an old standby at repelling many pests, from insects to mammals, mothballs are not without their drawbacks. They are flammable, evaporate quickly (and therefore need frequent replacement), and are toxic to humans and pets. Inhaling the fumes can cause headaches, nausea, and vomiting. Restrict their use and carefully monitor the effects.

Creosote

This smelly black wood preservative used on utility poles or railroad ties causes deer to turn up their noses and move on.

TO USE: Soak absorbent cotton rags in the thick oily substance and hang them about the yard or garden. Wear rubber gloves to keep it off your hands. Tap garden stakes into the ground at strategic intervals, about six feet apart, and drape the soggy rags over the tops of the stakes. A heavy-duty rubber band around the top of the rag will hold it in place. Be careful not to let the creosote touch your skin or clothing, as it stains forever.

PROS AND CONS: It's messy. It's stinky, especially in hot weather. But creosote does work, especially when staked next to particularly vulnerable plants. Used primarily for industrial purposes, it may be difficult to find for consumer purchase.

Creosote waste from home use is not considered a hazardous material, but in the quantities generated from industrial use it is treated very seriously. Don't burn the rags once you're finished with them; send them to the landfill.

Processed Sewage

Here's a plus. Fertilize your garden and keep deer away in one step. Tests have found that in areas of low deer pressure, yards treated with fertilizers derived from processed sewage were apparently considered repugnant by deer. Although no gardeners reported using concentrated fish fertilizer as a deer deterrent, one would expect that fragrant brew to work in much the same way. The heavy, lingering scent ought to be enough to repel anything that can walk away.

To use: Top-dress or work into the soil. Foliar feeding (diluting and spraying directly onto foliage) boosts plant nutrition in addition to providing a simultaneous coating of smell.

Pros and cons: The good news is that using a sewage-based fertilizer reduces two chores to one. The bad news, as with many repellents, is that it works best in areas of low-to-average deer pressure. Hungry deer hold their noses and ignore it.

Related commercial product: Milorganite.

Blood Meal and Dried Blood

A "red alert" repellent, blood meal has long been recommended as a deer deterrent, as well as advocated by organic gardeners as a plant food. Blood products are high in nitrogen (12 to 15 percent) and phosphorus (1.3 to 3 percent). Blood meal also contains about 1 percent potash. Though probably less effective than some other deterrents, blood products are nonetheless a useful addition to the deer-proofing arsenal. The message from this scent to deer is very likely one of "others have shed their blood here — *beware*."

To use: For shrubs or trees, make small pouches of old nylons or cloth and fill them with blood meal. The bags need not be placed nearly as close together as soap or fabric softener strips

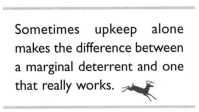

Sometimes upkeep alone makes the difference between a marginal deterrent and one that really works.

because the odor sends a more menacing message. The odor of the dried meal isn't very noticeable, but once the meal gets wet it reeks of danger to deer. Create a barrier around your yard by hanging the pouches of meal around the perimeter, or simply place them in and around vulnerable plants. You can also top-dress beds or rows with it, which gives your plants a free lunch. Feather meal, a by-product of the poultry processing industry, can be used in the same way.

As an alternative, reconstitute dried blood with water and spray on and around foliage.

PROS AND CONS: Blood meal and dried blood provide a measure of control while benefiting garden growth. The biggest shortcoming is the need for vigilance: The meal degrades and washes away, and the blood spray must be regularly reapplied. Sometimes upkeep alone makes the difference between a marginal deterrent and one that really works.

Be aware that blood products may attract predators, from coyotes and rats to dogs and cats, into the garden.

Bone Tar Oil

An effective deer deterrent, bone tar oil also repels other potential garden raiders. It undoubtedly carries much the same message to the deer as blood meal.

TO USE: Tear strips of absorbent cloth or cut cord or rope into one- or two-foot lengths. Pour the oil into an old container that you won't mind throwing away, then saturate the cloth or cord in it. Do this away from the house and wear rubber gloves. Tie or otherwise secure the soaked material to stakes placed near vulnerable plants.

PROS AND CONS: Two words: P. U. This is one of those repellents that, once you experience it for yourself, you need not ask how it works. Another drawback is that bone tar oil does not weather all that well and like many other repellents needs to be, um, freshened fairly frequently.

RELATED COMMERCIAL PRODUCT: Magic Circle.

Tankage

See pages 114–116, "Tactics NOT to Try."

Predator Urine or Feces

Among the most powerful of the "red alert" repellents is the overwhelming odor of predator urine or feces. The fresh droppings of such natural predators as cougars, coyotes, bobcats, bears, and wolves constitute an undeniable warning that deer instinctively avoid. The odors of predators that North American deer would never encounter in the wild, such as lions, tigers, hyenas, and polar bears, are just as effective. Many researchers, including those at the Connecticut State Agricultural Experiment Station, have confirmed what the deer already knew: Predators scare away prey.

There's no need to stalk the woods with a pooper-scooper. Nearby zoos are the best source of predator urine and feces. Best because someone else has to collect the stuff; all the gardener has to do is bring it home and set it out. Also, you might be surprised at how many people own large cats as pets. And wolves and wolf hybrids have become an unfortunate fad of the nineties. Owners are usually relieved to have someone haul away their pets' by-products.

TO USE: Be sure to secure a source of *fresh* urine or feces. The aromatic properties break down quickly, and samples only a few days old have lost considerable potency. Store in an airtight, plastic container in a cool, dark place.

Containers of urine or feces fare better in the garden than merely plopping it down here and there. The container concentrates the odor and protects it from wind, rain, and other disturbances. Small plastic tubs that held, for example, margarine or cottage cheese work well. Poke lots of holes along the sides to let those heady aromas waft through, and place the containers along the perimeters of the garden or near especially vulnerable plants.

PROS AND CONS: Predator urine or feces can be an effective deer deterrent as long as you replenish it often. For many gardeners the most difficult aspect of using them is *finding* them in the first place. Also, gathering, storing, and handling these substances is not for the faint of heart or nose. As a side benefit, predator scents repel a range of creatures that feast upon your garden, from mice to moose.

RELATED COMMERCIAL PRODUCTS: Commercial outlets for predator urine and feces are listed in the Appendix.

BAD TASTES

Taste repellents work differently from odor repellents. Rather than forming an odor barrier to an *area*, taste repellents, also called contact repellents, protect the exact plant or leaf to which you spray, brush, or otherwise apply them; deer must taste the repellent before it can take effect. This is both their greatest success and their biggest drawback. If *any* other food is available, deer can't stomach leaves or stems coated with such nasty stuff, but first they must *learn*. Unfortunately, learning means tasting and tasting means at least a little bit of damage. Most deer will try several bites before they realize that the entire plant (or border, or garden) tastes awful.

> Plants you have treated to taste bad to deer won't taste good to you either.

For gardeners who enjoy deer in or near their yards, contact repellents may be the perfect answer. Deer do not withdraw from the entire area. They may still meander through now and then, even once they decide you have nothing in your yard worth eating. But unless starvation threatens, your bitter bushes and sour grapes will not tempt them to taste again.

Just as area repellents have cons as well as pros, contact repellents have a few shortcomings of their own. First, most taste repellents are meant exclusively for nonfood plants: Plants you have treated to taste bad to the deer won't taste good to you either. Second, contact repellents protect only the parts of the plants they actually cover. Make sure to spray the entire plant, from the ground up to at least five or six feet high. Also, as with odors, tastes weather. The rate of reapplication varies with different repellents, but all require more than one dose, from occasional touch-ups to complete reapplication. Additional applications are necessary to protect new growth, the deer's favorite part of the plant, as foliage unfolds throughout the growing season.

Hot Pepper Spray

Not only does pepper spray taste bad, but also the active ingredient in hot peppers, capsaicin, *burns*. It is so potent that sprays containing it can ward off attacking dogs and grizzly bears. Once a deer gets a mouthful of treated foliage, you have to feel sorry for the poor beast. But it will do no real harm and the deer will definitely not make the same mistake twice.

To use: Whip up a batch of super-hot sauce in a bucket or tub and spray wherever needed. Such additives as Vapor Gard and Wilt-Pruf extend the life of the mixture, help it adhere to the foliage, and prevent drying out, but are not absolutely necessary if you don't mind frequent reapplications. Apply with a garden sprayer. Coating just those plants around the perimeter may stave off further exploration by nosy deer, or you may need to cover everything vulnerable.

Homemade hot pepper sprays are among the only taste repellents that can be used on crops. Don't apply just before harvest, and be sure to rinse foods thoroughly and test cautiously before eating any treated foods. For a produce spray, try either of these hot pepper spray recipes.

An important tip: Some plants may be very sensitive to hot sauce sprays. Test spray or dip a leaf or two in the concoction before dowsing the entire plant. Check after a few days for any discoloration or dead leaves. If all looks good, then treat the rest of the plant.

Pros and cons: Deer won't stage a repeat performance once they taste your spicy flavored flowers. Homemade sprays are cheap and effective, the only caution being that not only some plants, but also many pollinators, are sensitive to capsaicin. Homemade pepper sprays require regular reapplications after rainfall or overhead watering, unless you add an antidesiccant sticking agent, such as the products mentioned above.

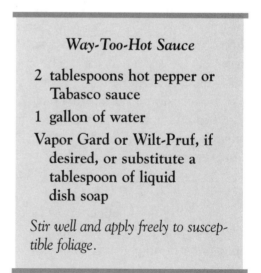

Way-Too-Hot Sauce

2 tablespoons hot pepper or Tabasco sauce

1 gallon of water

Vapor Gard or Wilt-Pruf, if desired, or substitute a tablespoon of liquid dish soap

Stir well and apply freely to susceptible foliage.

RELATED COMMERCIAL PRODUCTS: Hot Sauce Animal Repellent is labeled for use on shrubs, Christmas trees, fruit trees, and vegetables. It must be applied before the fruit set or vegetables develop. It's expensive, currently about $175 per gallon, but so concentrated that eight ounces will cover an acre.

Green Eggs and . . .

That's it. Putrid eggs. The same stuff that smells bad tastes worse. So while you're concocting Eau de Rotten Eggs (see page 93) as an area repellent, make enough to cover thoroughly any particularly vulnerable plants.

TO USE: Spray, drizzle, brush, or splatter over plants to be protected. If the smell doesn't keep deer away, the taste will.

PROS AND CONS: A double-duty deterrent, rotten egg mix very effectively dissuades deer. The smell becomes unnoticeable (to people) once the solution dries on foliage, but the taste remains. Rotten eggs should not be used on any plant meant for human consumption.

RELATED COMMERCIAL PRODUCTS: See under "Garlic and Rotten Eggs," above.

Soap Spray

Soapy water, especially when laced with human scent, serves as another double deterrent to deer. It not only smells bad, but also tastes atrocious to deer, according to a Wisconsin gardener who suggested this solution to the gray water disposal problem.

Too-Hot-to-Handle Spray

4–5 tablespoons cayenne pepper

1 gallon water

1 tablespoon vegetable oil

Mix well and spray where needed. You can substitute a handful of homegrown hot peppers (typically, the smaller, pointed, red-maturing varieties, such as habañero and cayenne) for the cayenne powder. Puree in blender and strain through cheesecloth.

TO USE: Save soapy bathwater or whip up a fresh batch of soapy water from bar soap. Spray on the foliage of vulnerable plants. Since some plants are sensitive to soap, be sure to test spray a patch before fully treating.

PROS AND CONS: Though his approach has not been thoroughly tested, the reporting Wisconsin gardener claims total success using his sudsy solution. Gray water offers the additional advantage of being free, the basis is reasonable (deer are repelled by soaps, and if you've ever had your mouth washed out with it, you know it tastes bad), and it can't do any harm. Drawbacks include the fact that you have to respray after a good rain or two. Also, soap leaves an unattractive whitish film on foliage and can attract rodents. If mice or similar varmints are a problem in your garden, stir in a tablespoon of hot pepper sauce.

RELATED COMMERCIAL PRODUCT: Hinder (see page 91).

Thiram

Originally developed as a seed protectant, the fungicide thiram has proved quite distasteful to deer. It irritates mucous membranes in and around the mouth and nostrils. Be sure to check the label and follow the instructions regarding which plants this (and any other commercial) product can be used on. Never apply commercial products to food crops unless they are specifically labeled as approved for those crops.

TO USE: Mix 1 part thiram with 1 to 2 parts water and spray on susceptible plants. Be sure to spray up to a height of at least six feet.

PROS AND CONS: Although apparently very effective in reducing deer damage, thiram has a couple of drawbacks. First, you should use it only on plants for which it is registered. Second, it can be applied only to dormant plants, and only when temperatures are above freezing. In addition, it costs about $50 to the acre.

RELATED COMMERCIAL PRODUCTS: You can purchase thiram in straight form as a fungicide and in animal repellent concentrations as Chew-Not and Rabbit-Deer Repellent.

Systemic Aversives

Systemic aversives, for lack of a simpler term, are substances absorbed through the root systems of plants to make them taste bad through and through. The best example, denatonium benzoate, is available commercially as No-Bite Tablets. Another formula, benzyl diethyl [2,6 xylylcarbamoyl] methyl ammonium saccharide and thymol (sold as Ro-Pel) has not performed as well in research trials.

TO USE: Bury one denatonium benzoate tablet near the roots of each plant to be protected. A single tablet should last from one to three years. Spray Ro-Pel over foliage according to the manufacturer's instructions. It can used to protect nursery stock, Christmas trees, annuals, perennials, and shrubs.

PROS AND CONS: Although simple to use, safe, and nontoxic, denatonium benzoate tablets are not inexpensive compared to other taste repellents: A supply of five hundred tablets rings up to about $275. As with other taste deterrents, the deer must sample the forbidden fruit before they learn the consequences. Though wonderful for ornamentals, this is obviously not an option for food crops.

STARTLING SIGHTS

No one has reported success keeping deer away using *only* visual deterrents, but in combination with other deterrents they can make an important contribution. In general, two or more senses always confirm a threat much more convincingly than a mere single-sense suspicion.

Anything visually new or strange will make deer instantly suspicious, but they get over it. Deer have what is known as a "flight distance." If something comes too close, they take flight. Oddly enough, however, if they don't notice something until it is already *within* their flight distance, they may ignore it. It's as if they

Deer have what is known as a "flight distance." If something comes too close, they take flight. But if something is already within their flight distance when they detect it, they may ignore it.

think, "Well, if you've gotten this close, you must be harmless. Otherwise I'd be gone by now."

This is why an old-fashioned scarecrow doesn't work very well on deer. They can't recognize a scarecrow as a human form much beyond a hundred paces, and once they get that close they may decide that it poses no threat. After the deer have seen the scarecrow a few times, it becomes part of the scenery. You can try moving a scarecrow every few days and dressing it in floppy clothes that wave in the breeze, but it still isn't terribly effective. But a visual deterrent that actively moves is another story. If your scarecrow suddenly jumps or waves its arms, the deer depart posthaste. Menacing movements make the difference.

Mechanical Gizmos

Whether you wind them up, pop in batteries, or plug them in, there are so many moving mechanical gizmos out there, from toy robots to overhead fans, that the only limits are what you have available (or how much you're willing to spend) and your imagination. Anything that suddenly moves will startle deer, especially if it was sitting there minding its own business before it jumped. If it advances in their direction, so much the better. When a predator scent or strange noise accompanies the beastie, the result is an effective scare.

To use: Be ingenious. With a little ingenuity any gardener can create, for example, his or her own version of Frankenstein's monster to stand sentry. Give it some erratically moving parts and watch the deer stand back. One innovative gardener in Texas reports a scarecrow that has been successfully standing guard duty for seven months. Her secret? She scented the scarecrow's clothes with deodorant soap and attached movable eyes.

Pros and cons: Any moving mechanical gizmo will probably frighten deer from your yard, at least initially. But if the deer learn that the thing can't catch them, they won't run away from it. Your best hope may be that they won't return after the initial encounter.

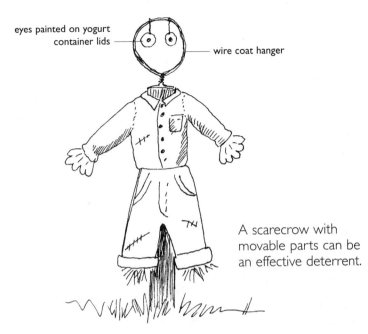

eyes painted on yogurt container lids

wire coat hanger

A scarecrow with movable parts can be an effective deterrent.

RELATED COMMERCIAL PRODUCTS: Mechanical scarecrows sold for orchard protection are available in several models.

White Flags

Grazing peacefully at meadow's edge, the group of deer suddenly tenses. The atmosphere changes in an instant from one of pastoral peace to adrenaline-charged anxiety. One doe stamps a foot, another turns towards the woods, but when a third raises that white flag aloft, all bound for cover. What was it? Who knows? But whatever the source of the scare, the message was in that waving white flag.

TO USE: Fashion white flags from white cloth or rags. Flags about ten inches long and five or six inches wide mimic those of the real McCoy. Position the phony tails at strategic locations around the garden. Tie them to posts, branches, or fencing so that they will wave in the breeze. One clever gardener fastened monofilament (a ten-dollar word for fishing line) to the end of two white rags tied close to his front porch.

As he kept watch, two deer stepped nearer and nearer a cherished rosebush. He tugged on the line and the two fake white tails shot up and bounced around. The two true whitetails didn't hang around long enough to find out what the trouble was.

PROS AND CONS: White flags are meaningless to blacktails or mule deer, and eventually whitetails will probably get wise to the fact that those other "deer" don't actually run away. If used with additional deterrents, however, white flags confirm a nervous deer's suspicions that danger lurks nearby. If you want to try the fishing line technique, consider purchasing a monitoring device that will alert you when something has entered your yard.

Floodlights

Neither gardeners nor wildlife biologists seem to be able to agree on whether or not lighting makes a difference to dining deer. After all, it's not ambience they seek.

Floodlights can be timed to go on at irregular intervals or programmed to a motion detector.

TO USE: Install floodlights so that the beam shines into the yard. Plug them in and see what happens.

PROS AND CONS: Motion-sensor lights rank high on the list of things insurance companies like to see in your yard anyway, so for the sake of home security alone they are a good investment. Although relatively inexpensive and easy to install and operate, they lose their effectiveness as a deterrent as soon as the deer figure out that nothing changes except the lighting.

RELATED COMMERCIAL PRODUCT: Blast Away Deer solar-powered floodlight.

OFFENSIVE SOUNDS

Imagine being deep in the forest, the ground soft and scented of humus. Raindrops fall, leaves rustle in the breeze. Birds, mice, and squirrels scamper and call. You are enveloped in small, muted sounds and thick, familiar scents. Between heartbeats something changes. A tick of a watch, the crunch of brittle leaves a hundred yards away, and you are gone. Classic behavior. If you're a deer.

A deer's sense of hearing is vital to its every action. Watch those radarlike ears swivel and then suddenly focus, and it's obvious that they are listening to everything around them. Having learned which sounds are "normal" in their world, deer filter them out, but they instantly detect and quickly evaluate the smallest "wrong" sound. They may stare in the direction of the noise, ears cocked full forward. They may stamp a forefoot or advance toward the sound in an effort to force any hiding predator to betray its whereabouts. Or they may immediately flee for safety.

In urban and suburban areas deer have long realized that we humans are a noisy lot, and frightening them away with sound may not be as easy as in quiet country settings. The deer must perceive the sound as a genuine threat.

Shake, Rattle, and Roll

Like most of the best deterrents, those that shake, rattle, and roll actually assault more than one sense, in this case sight and hearing. Pie pans, planks, strings of tin cans, and so forth have been a staple in the gardener's arsenal for generations.

TO USE: There are limitless possibilities here. The idea is to hang, by twine or invisible monofilament, something that moves and rattles in the breeze. Examples include:

- *Aluminum pie pans:* String them over susceptible plants in pairs. As the pie pans move with the wind, they not only clank together, but the motion and sporadic glare from the shiny surfaces also create a visual deterrent.
- *Tin cans on a string:* Tie tin cans in bunches and hang these clattering wind chimes about the garden.

♦ *Scraps of metal roofing, fiberglass siding, or old planks:* Drill a hole at one end of a scrap about six inches wide and three feet long. Thread heavy twine or rope through and hang in a tree or other spot where the scrap will bump and rattle with the wind. Every few days, move the deterrent to a fresh location in the yard.

PROS AND CONS: A time-honored, inexpensive deer deterrent that makes good use of materials on hand. Such devices do fend off deer, for a while, but are somewhat labor intensive to set up and move around, and as the season wears on the deer will get used to them. Taking them down entirely while employing a separate set of deterrents, then reinstalling them, works best.

Radios

Whether it's talk radio or hard rock, the sounds carried by radio waves are not soothing to deer. Until they get used to them, deer find those sounds very unnerving. But therein lies the rub, for get used to them they will.

TO USE: Some people recommend tuning the radio *between* stations to make the sounds as erratic, high pitched, and annoying as possible. Considering that deer hear in a much higher range than people (up to thirty thousand cycles per

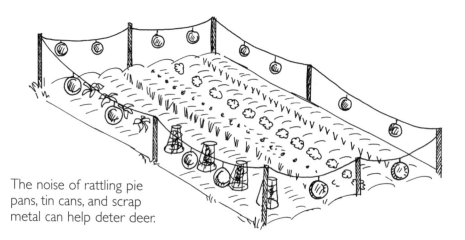

The noise of rattling pie pans, tin cans, and scrap metal can help deter deer.

second, compared to the human average of fifteen thousand), the squelches and squeals may be more noticeable to them, but that does not necessarily mean they will interpret the noise as dangerous. Other folks swear that talk radio, especially a heated debate, with rising and falling, emotional human voices, offers the best deterrent. Still others claim that deer find more frightening the crashing crescendos of classical music or the violent beats of hard rock.

Tune the radio as you see fit, turn up the volume, and place it in the garden before dusk. Let it play all night or, if it has an alarm, set it to begin playing just before peak deer activity. Protect the radio from the weather by placing it under an overhang or inside a waterproof container with at least one open side — a five-gallon plastic bucket turned on its side will suffice. Move the radio around from night to night to prolong the period of effectiveness. Changing stations or frequencies periodically may help.

PROS AND CONS: Strange sounds and/or human voices emanating from the greenery are sure to disturb deer, but probably not for long. And who else will the radio disturb? Neither you nor your neighbors should have to lose sleep over deer in your yard. If, however, you can play the radio loudly in good conscience, by all means add it to your repertoire. It's clean, it doesn't smell bad, and it just might keep the deer away from the garden for a few more days.

Things That Go Boom

Nothing beats a sudden loud blast for sending deer scattering from the scene in a hurry. Propane or gas cannons and sonic bombs work well. They generally protect an area of from five to ten acres, making them most useful for commercial sites, such as nursery tree plantings, orchards, or large crops.

TO USE: Be sure to follow the manufacturer's guidelines regarding fuel, setup, and maintenance. Position the noisemaker near the center of the area that needs protection and set it to go off at desired intervals. Regularly alter the timing between blasts to prolong the effectiveness.

PROS AND CONS: Your neighbors may *never* speak to you again, unless they too suffer from unbearable deer damage. Before resorting to such a measure, meet with any neighbors within cannon shot and discuss your concerns. If they share your deer problem they may even offer to foot some of the bill, as the exploders can run into the hundreds of dollars. (Wildlife agencies sometimes have them for rent or loan to private individuals.) The booms will scare away birds as well as deer, and probably other wildlife as well, but deer become accustomed to the noise in about a month.

RELATED COMMERCIAL PRODUCTS: High-pitched sonic warning devices can also be purchased from various outlets (see Appendix).

Snap, Crackle, Pop

A smaller version of the loud boom is the snap, crackle, or pop. A slow-burning string of firecrackers will startle deer away from an area.

TO USE: Attach a string of firecrackers to a long, slow-burning fuse and light before retiring or leaving the garden for the day. If you string the firecrackers out along an extended length of rope, they will go off randomly over a period of time.

PROS AND CONS: Because firecrackers constitute a fire and safety hazard, many places ban them. Check your local ordinances. Here again, the noise may be more of a nuisance than the deer, and using firecrackers requires vigilance to make sure neighborhood kids stay away from them and that nothing catches fire.

Whistles

One sound well known to all who live in deer country is the short, loud snort that signals danger. One deer clears its sinuses and they all take off. Whistles designed to copy this signal are available for mounting on vehicles in an attempt to avert collisions.

TO USE: Follow the manufacturer's guidelines for installation and use.

PROS AND CONS: As for preventing collisions, insurance companies believe in the whistles even though wildlife biologists don't. The concept is a sound one, so to speak, for garden use, even though not yet widely adopted. As an alternative, create a loud tape-recorded version of the "snort" to play at random.

Ultrasound

High tech comes to gardening. A variety of ultrasonic devices are available. According to the manufacturers, deer (and other animals) find high-pitched frequencies intolerable. Since, by definition, humans can't hear ultrasound, it offers the benefit of annoying only the animals. At least one commercially available unit is motion activated, which should make it more effective than a constant or predictable pattern of sound.

TO USE: Follow the manufacturer's recommendations. Remember, sound waves emitted from a speaker travel in a straight line away from their point of origin. If anything comes between the emitter and the intended recipient, the recipient won't receive. So be sure to position the machine so that it faces the area of your yard most likely to be damaged by deer.

PROS AND CONS: A clean, quiet box that you plug in, and the deer stay away. Such a wonderful premise, but insufficient reports exist to verify the success of ultrasonic machines.

SURPRISE TOUCHES

Nothing alarms a wild animal more than something unseen that reaches out and grabs it. To a deer a surprise touch offers a glimpse of certain death. If the grab carries a physical shock, the more impact the encounter will have on the deer's future behavior.

> To a deer, a surprise touch offers a glimpse of certain death.

Monofilament

The humble fishing line has found a new set of admirers. And a set of Cervidae that abhor the stuff, even though they have no concept of what it is. The long-harried gardener has one more cheap, effective tool for his arsenal, and the deer have one more unseen, confounding deterrent.

TO USE: Again, magazine readerships have contributed to the field of deer deterrence. A note in *Field & Stream* led the editors of *Hortideas* to ask their readers to try using monofilament as a means of barring deer. The original idea was to string eight or nine strands around an area as an invisible barrier. It was thought that deer would bump into this mysterious wall and retreat in confusion. At least one reader of *Hortideas* responded that *a single strand* of heavy deep-sea fishing line was all it took to spook the deer from his yard.

String the line at a height of from two to three feet. The deer walk into it, can't see it or comprehend what it could be, and withdraw to safer territory.

PROS AND CONS: Monofilament is not expensive and may even be had for free, as the reader of *Hortideas* suggests. He recommends checking with sporting goods stores that replace old line for their customers. They may have a spool of the old stuff they would happily give away. (But don't waste your time unraveling tangled-up wads of old line.) On the negative side, the thin line may be difficult for the gardener as well as the deer to spot. It can be embarrassing to trip over something you put up in the first place, and downright frustrating to try and work or mow around. But all in all, this is one of the most promising tactics to try.

The Electric Strand

If deer find it very discomforting to walk into something unseen, they find it all the more discomforting if the "something" carries the sharp, sudden pang of an electric shock.

TO USE: Electric fence wire is sold in reels at hardware or feed stores. String the wire around the perimeter of the yard and attach one end to a grounding rod that you pound into the ground. String the other end through a plastic insulator attached to a tree, stake, or post. Wire the fence to an electric

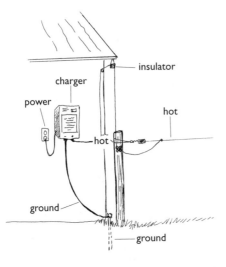

Key components of an electric strand include electric fence wire, an insulator, a grounding rod, and a charger.

fence charger. Be sure to follow manufacturer's instructions and to keep the charger (unless it is a weatherproof solar model) under cover from the elements. When a deer touches the wire it completes the electrical circuit and suffers the consequences. (For more information about setting up electrified fencing, see the next chapter.)

PROS AND CONS: An electric strand is lightweight, flexible, easy to install, nearly invisible when in place, and surprisingly effective at deterring unsuspecting deer. The greatest expense is for the electric charger. Some deer, however, especially in times or areas of extreme deer pressure, will brave the shock or learn to clear the strand. Periodically altering the location or height of the wire helps tremendously.

Snow cover, which can insulate the deer from the ground, may disable an electric strand even if the wire itself remains above the snow.

Notify neighbors, especially those with small children, that your property is guarded by electrified wire. Consider turning the charger on only from dusk till morning, when deer activity is greatest and child activity lowest.

Timed Sprinklers

What suddenly jumps up from the ground, hisses and spits, and splatters unsuspecting deer? Sprinklers set off by timers or, better yet, linked to motion detectors. The sounds and feel of water spraying at them have sent many deer scampering from estate and park lawns. But, ever adaptable, the deer soon learn the sprinkler schedule. So make the schedule unlearnable.

TO USE: For existing in-ground systems, merely program the sprinklers to go on and off at odd intervals during peak deer feeding times. If you don't have in-ground sprinklers, you can achieve the same effect inexpensively by attaching a sprinkler timer (available at garden centers) to an outdoor faucet or hydrant, screwing on a garden hose, and connecting a sprinkler at the opposite end. Motion detectors can be linked to sprinklers for custom watering.

PROS AND CONS: From costly to cheap, this is one of those deterrents that can't really lose. Even if the deer aren't spooked, the yard gets watered.

TACTICS **NOT** TO TRY

Over the years a lot of desperate gardeners have tried a lot of desperate means to keep deer away. The worse the situation, the more drastic the tactics employed. But there are limits to what we could and should try, as individuals, to alleviate a landscape or gardening problem.

In some cases the limits have been defined by law. In others, the experiences of those who have gone before us, or plain old common sense, should tell us we have crossed the line. If your deer problem is so intense that you would seriously consider such extreme tactics as poisoning and shooting, then the situation has mushroomed beyond a gardening concern and become an issue of wildlife management and public policy (see Chapter 7, "Community Efforts").

Really Repugnant Repellents

The list of odor repellents suggested earlier in this chapter probably seemed eclectic to some readers, but those with successful deer-deterring experience may have recognized them as rather mundane compared to some that have been tried by some gardeners.

Many sources recommend acquiring tankage, the putrefied cast-off bits and pieces from slaughterhouses, for use in the garden. While the stench does keep deer away, there are serious drawbacks. In rural areas the odor attracts predators, from magpies to coyotes and on up the food chain. In suburban areas dogs and cats become real nuisances trying to get at the reeking ingredients. Consider also that spoiled, rotting meat and innards are loaded with bacteria, from *E. coli* to who-knows-what. None of which you need multiplying in your garden. Rainwater or the overhead sprinkler could splash some very nasty germs from tankage onto food crops. Finally, the smell is just too awful.

Another so-called clever idea is that using human urine or feces will keep deer away. Could be true, but if you try it, please don't invite me over. While urine is sterile and loaded with nitrogen, the smell is drawback enough for most people. Human waste left out in the garden violates public health laws and is incredibly unsanitary. Again, germs abound and you don't want to give them free access to your garden.

Habitat Modification

First of all, unless you *own* the land, attempting to modify deer habitat could get you into some serious trouble with landowners. Moreover, destroying woody cover that deer prefer also eliminates habitat for other wildlife, from songbirds to chipmunks.

Given the mobility of deer, to effect any noticeable difference in deer traffic the altered habitat area would have to be measured by the square mile, not in acres. In the end, attempting to reduce deer damage by altering their habitat is not worth the financial or environmental cost, and the word from researchers is that it just doesn't work.

Poisoning

Stated simply, don't. No poisons are registered in the United States for deer control. Poisoning deer with any substance for any reason is *illegal*. No matter how big a pest a deer has become in your yard, death by poisoning is an undeserved, hideous end.

Trapping

Wildlife officials sometimes trap and remove nuisance deer, usually to relocate them. Such devices as rocket nets, drop-door box traps, and tranquilizer guns are used to catch deer with as little trauma as possible. Officials then transport the captured animals to an area of lower deer population.

Unfortunately, research reveals that relocated deer do not fend well. In a recent study, only two of fifteen tagged and relocated deer survived a full year. Add to that the exorbitant cost of capturing and moving deer, and the consensus is that the result seldom justifies live removal.

Traps set up to kill deer are illegal.

Shooting

With the exception of legally sanctioned hunts or special depredation-control permits, it is illegal to shoot deer. Sitting on the porch firing off a few rounds into the garden doesn't qualify as hunting, and, in the context of the civilization we live in, isn't defensible. Deer are protected under the law as a game species, and states prosecute anyone shooting deer illegally.

Deer Deterrents at a Glance

Deterrent	Longevity*	Relative Cost	Comments
Repellents			
Soap	Several weeks	Low per individual tree; moderate per square foot	Very easy to use
Hair	Few weeks	Free	Very easy to use
Repellent plants	Indefinite	Low to moderate	Avoid toxic plants
Garlic, rotten egg	Few weeks	Free to low	Smells bad during preparation; application easy to messy
Fabric softener	Until hard rain	Moderate	Very easy to use
Mothballs	Few weeks	Moderate to expensive	Avoid fumes, skin contact
Creosote	Several weeks	Moderate, if available	Messy to apply; take care with disposal
Processed sewage	Several weeks	Moderate	Very easy to use; commercial products may contain heavy metals
Blood meal	Days to few weeks	Moderate	May attract predators
Bone tar oil	Few weeks	Low	Hold your nose
Predator urine	Days to weeks	Free to moderate	Challenging to acquire
Hot pepper spray	Days to weeks	Free to low	Don't apply to food plants within one week of harvest
Egg spray	Days to weeks	Free to low	Requires preparation
Soap spray	Days to few weeks	Free to low	Easy to use
Thiram	Weeks	Moderate	Follow product label
Systemic aversives	Indefinitely	Moderate to expensive	Don't use on food crops

Deterrent	Longevity*	Relative Cost	Comments
Other Deterrents			
White flags	Weeks	Low	Works only for whitetails
Mechanical gizmos	Weeks	Free to moderate	Easy to use; may require assembly
Floodlights	Weeks	Moderate to expensive	Requires installation
Homemade noisemakers	Weeks	Free to moderate	Requires assembly
Radios	Weeks	Moderate to expensive	Very easy to use
Propane cannons, sonic bombs, sonic warning devices	Weeks	Expensive	Require installation and tolerant neighbors
Firecrackers	Weeks	Moderate	May be a fire or health hazard
Deer whistles	Weeks	Moderate to expensive	Questionable effectiveness
Ultrasound	Indefinite	Moderate to expensive	Questionable effectiveness
Monofilament	Days to weeks	Low	Watch where you walk
Electric strand	Weeks	Moderate	May be a hazard to children
Timed sprinklers	Indefinite	Moderate to expensive	Remember when they start!

* Longevity is relative to many factors, especially, for repellents, weather conditions. In general, repellents with longevities of "several weeks" will last somewhat longer than those with longevities of "few weeks," conditions being equal. For other deterrents, longevity is largely a function of how quickly the deer adapt to the particular technique.

6 Fencing Lessons

There are many who believe the *only* way to keep deer out is with fencing. And not just any fencing, mind you, but the type that costs hundreds of dollars or more and looks like a prison barricade. My garden in Elk, Washington, had such a fence — eight to ten feet high in places, constructed of pine poles and woven sheep wire, and topped with two strands of barbed wire. At least one deer still got in. It probably crawled under a gap in the wire.

Regardless of the type of fencing you choose, it will be most effective if you build it before deer damage starts. If possible, install fencing prior to putting in expensive landscape plantings or before you plant your vegetable garden in the spring. Unless deer realize there's a reason to cross a fence, they won't put the effort into doing it.

To understand what kind of fencing it really takes to keep deer out, consider their physical limitations. Which are few. Any healthy deer can clear a five-foot tall fence without even trying. Most can vault six or seven feet, and some can breeze over an eight-footer. Deer can also take wide spans in stride.

They have been observed clearing streams fourteen feet wide, with room to spare. One limitation they do have is that they cannot perform a high jump *and* a broad jump all in one manuever.

Another factor that limits which fences a deer will test is the landing site. Deer will not jump without a reasonable expectation that a safe landing awaits. Accomplished leapers that they are, they know the inherent damage of a bad landing and avoid putting themselves at risk.

> ### Three Quick Fencing Lessons
>
> *Lesson One:* Fence first, plant second.
> *Lesson Two:* If deer can't go over, through, or under, they'll go around.
> *Lesson Three:* A fence with a hole is no fence at all.

It's a fairly common mistake to fence the yard incompletely. Many people leave the driveway open, or a view side of the property or some other gap in an otherwise flawless fence. This approach actually works for a while with whitetailed deer, which tend to stick to their established pathways. If these paths are barricaded, it may take the deer a few days to formulate an alternate plan. But only a few days — at best. Once deer have made your yard a regular stop, they'll find their way through or around such a fence.

What constitutes an incomplete fence? A twelve-inch gap in a fence is room enough for determined deer to squeeze through. If they can find no way around or through, then the deer look for a way to get under. If you haven't partially buried or pegged your fence to the ground, deer can wriggle beneath.

If you combine all these considerations, the logical conclusion is that an effective fence, besides being installed before deer damage starts, must be high, a combination of high and wide, or solid enough to obscure potential landing sites. And, of course, it must be impenetrable.

NONELECTRIC FENCES

The following nonelectric fences, tested in the field by researchers and gardeners, have proved effective under the conditions noted for each. The intention here is not to provide you with all the information you need to actually *build* a fence — for that you should consult a fencing how-to book, such as Gail Damerow's *Fences for Pasture & Garden* (Pownal, Vermont: Garden Way Publishing, 1992), and local fence builders. But you should come away from this discussion and the subsequent section on electric fences with a clearer idea of what will meet your needs.

Standard Deer Fence

The standard deer fence is a tall, sturdy fence constructed of woven wire and built at least eight feet tall. The wire can be "hog wire" or "sheep wire" with openings up to six inches square, or (more expensive) "horse wire" in which the openings are about two by four inches. Some gardeners resort to "chicken wire," with openings of one or two inches. Woven wire is stronger than welded wire and more often recommended for

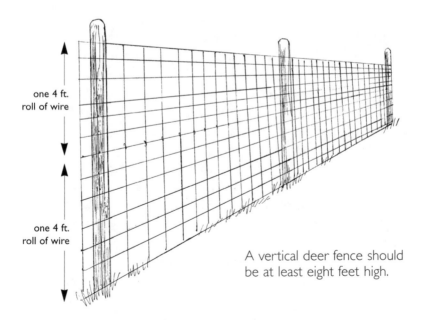

one 4 ft. roll of wire

one 4 ft. roll of wire

A vertical deer fence should be at least eight feet high.

fencing in livestock, which tend to lean on or rub against fences. Welded wire may suffice for deer.

The wire comes in large, heavy rolls in varying lengths and widths. Hog wire typically comes in four-foot widths, making two widths necessary to construct an effective deer fence. A second width is attached atop the first (see illustration), and a row or two of single-strand wire is often attached above that. If possible, the bottom width should be partially buried or, at the very least, pegged down at intervals to prevent deer from squeezing under.

Since posts must be buried three to four feet deep to stabilize this fence, it requires twelve-foot-tall posts and lots of digging. Be sure to purchase pressure-treated posts for the greatest longevity.

PROS AND CONS: This type of fence, the most expensive to build and the most long-lasting, is very effective even where deer pressure is high. But such fences make their own landscape statement and may be too conspicuous for many homeowners.

Slanted Deer Fence

The slanted style of fence takes advantage of the fact that although deer can clear the height *or* the width of the fence, they cannot clear *both*. Often deer walk underneath the overhang and don't even realize there is a way over the fence. A single width of four-foot wire fencing, supplemented by several rows of single strands across the upper reaches of the overhang, is usually adequate. The fence should meet the ground at an angle of about forty-five degrees.

Recommended for areas with from moderate to high deer pressure, a slanted fence protects large areas well. High-tensile wire can be used instead of standard smooth or barbless wire to add an electrical shock to an otherwise already formidable barrier.

PROS AND CONS: The cost of construction is still substantial, but so is the life expectancy of the finished fence. While such fences need not be nearly as high as standard deer fences,

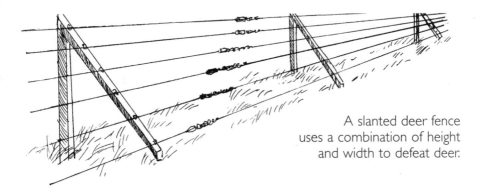

A slanted deer fence uses a combination of height and width to defeat deer.

they take up about six feet of horizontal space, which in some settings is unacceptable.

Double-Row Fence

To take advantage of the deer's inability to clear the high, wide, and mighty, construct two smaller fences side by side. This design also plays on the deer's fear of leaping without landing. The fences need only be four to five feet tall, and should be placed four to five feet apart.

PROS AND CONS: Why choose two when one will do? Because unlike a slanted fence, a double-row fence doesn't waste space. You can landscape or garden the median because the deer don't attempt to clear *either* fence.

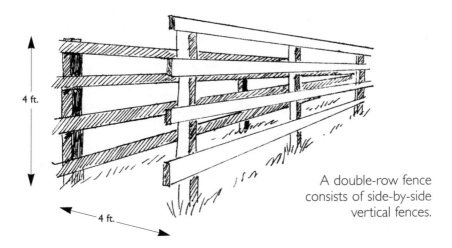

4 ft.

4 ft.

A double-row fence consists of side-by-side vertical fences.

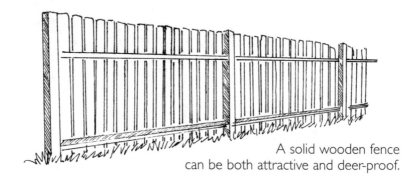

A solid wooden fence can be both attractive and deer-proof.

Those who have tried them give double fences rave reviews. The lower fence height makes it easier to construct than the standard eight-foot deer fence, but it does require more labor and twice the number of posts.

Converting an Upright Fence

If you happen to already have an upright fence in place that isn't quite tall enough to prevent deer from jumping over, convert it to a deer-proof fence. One option is to just keep going up, extending the posts with lashed or bolted poles or boards and attaching another width of woven wire. If you choose to use multiple rows of single-strand wire instead of mesh, the rows should be no more than four to six inches apart. Another option is to attach the post extensions at an

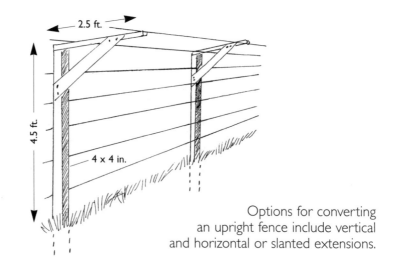

2.5 ft.

4.5 ft.

4 x 4 in.

Options for converting an upright fence include vertical and horizontal or slanted extensions.

angle, either horizontally or at forty-five degrees. The first option takes advantage of the deer's height limitations, whereas the two angled designs create a combined high-broad jump.

PROS AND CONS: Converting an existing fence eliminates wasting what was already there, which cuts the costs of construction considerably. Wood fences are easier to alter than steel, as steel must be bolted or welded. The original fence must be solid and stable. Don't try to extend a fence that has already outlived its usefulness.

Opaque Deer Fence

When is a five-foot-tall, single-width fence sufficient to keep deer on their own side? When they can't see over, through, or around it. Privacy fences look great and can take advantage of this simple principle. Just be sure that the fence has no gaps, such as loose gates or missing boards, that may invite the deer in.

PROS AND CONS: Solid fences can be constructed of various materials, from attractive cedar or redwood, to rough wood slabs, to leftover tags of sheet metal or fiberglass. The costs vary accordingly. The wooden fences offer the added benefit of attractive privacy, but if you define a beautiful fence as one that keeps deer out, any material will do. A fence of salvage material can be painted to make it more appealing, or you can camouflage it by planting climbing vines that deer will not eat.

Prefab Deer Netting

At last! New to the gardening market are sturdy plastic meshes made especially for deer control. As such, they have many advantages over bird netting and standard fencing materials. Made from black plastic, the mesh blends into a varied background extremely well, making it especially suitable for landscape protection.

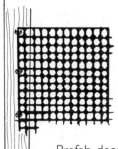

Prefab deer netting may be the easiest solution to your deer problem.

The plastic mesh was designed to be installed in several different ways, making it convenient for varied settings. It can be stretched from tree to tree or between treated posts of varying size and strength. The stability of the supports dictates how far apart they can be placed. You can buy specially made pegs for anchoring the netting to the ground in order to prevent the deer from squirming underneath, but in a pinch, bent coat hangers will do the trick.

Instructions for installing the fence recommend attaching white flags to it at a height of four feet, at twelve-foot intervals. This warns the deer that an otherwise invisible barrier has been installed and takes advantage of the "white flag" signal. After a month or two, the instructions advise, the flags can be removed because the deer will have become familiar with the fence and altered their routes accordingly.

PROS AND CONS: Lightweight, less expensive, and easier to install than livestock fencing, the plastic mesh blends into the landscape. Although strong enough to withstand deer pushing against it, the mesh will give if hit at an all-out run. A great solution to the deer invasion problem.

ELECTRIC FENCES

Electric fences deserve a few words of both praise and caution. Although useful and effective at deterring deer, livestock, and other pests, they carry with them a margin of liability. Municipalities frown on them, even though the fence chargers built today utilize low impedance and are capable of delivering only a harmless jolt, unlike the shocking monsters of the past. Some areas outlaw them outright. Know your local ordinances before erecting any type of electric fence.

Electric fences offer three distinct advantages over non-electric types:

* They are inexpensive. The labor and materials to construct an effective electric fence are generally much less than to build an equally effective non-electric fence.

- They "teach" the deer to avoid the area. One good zap and the deer head for friendlier territory.

- They can be made either temporary or permanent, depending on the situation.

Electrifying the Fence

Electric fence chargers vary in cost and the length of fence they can electrify, but all are regulated as to how much shock they can deliver. "Hot" fence chargers, which used to be common, are no longer sold because they presented a fire threat. Solar-powered chargers can be set up independent of any other power source, which makes them very useful in outlying areas of the yard or property.

The fence charger must be protected from the elements and installed where there is no danger of mechanical damage or of starting a fire, and, of course, where children and animals can't reach it. Another consideration is positioning the charger near an electrical outlet. It's best to plug the charger directly into the outlet, rather than to run an extension cord between charger and power source.

To work, all electric fences must be grounded. For the grounding system to achieve optimum performance, manufacturers typically recommend driving at least three grounding rods (more if the fence is long), each about six feet long, into the ground about ten feet from each other. The rods are then connected to one another and the fence by a continuous wire.

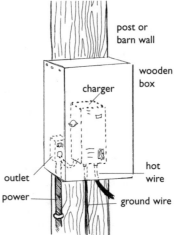

A fence charger must be sheltered and should be plugged directly into an outlet. Always consult the manufacturer's instructions before wiring a charger to your fence.

Electric fences use one of two basic shocking systems. In the first, an "earth-return" system, the current passes from a

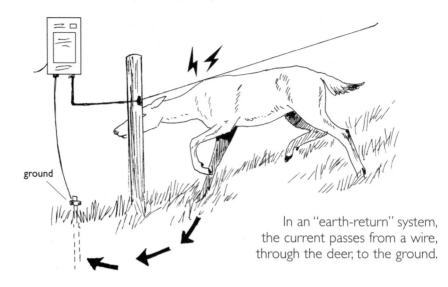

In an "earth-return" system, the current passes from a wire, through the deer, to the ground.

live wire, through the animal, and into the ground. From there it travels to the grounding rods and then back to the charger, completing the electrical circuit. This type of system works best in areas where the soil is relatively moist year-round.

Dry soil requires a different type of shocking system. Because dry soil disperses current more erratically than moist soil, it requires a "wire-return" system that doesn't rely on the conductivity of the soil. This system delivers a shock when an animal touches two wires, one live, the other grounded. Some electric fence designs call for electrified wires placed as high as five feet above the ground. Chances are that if a deer hits the fence at this point, the deer is airborne (not grounded) — another case where a wire-return system is the best bet.

Installation and Operation

Before constructing any electric fence, be sure the path of the fence is clear of all tall grass, weeds, brush, or other debris that might accidentally come into contact with the elecrified wires. String a strand of twine or wire between two end posts to serve as a guide to ensure a straight fence line. Set or drive fence posts about fifteen to twenty feet apart, depending on the terrain. Once the posts are in place, attach nonconductive insulators (made expressly for this purpose and sold wherever

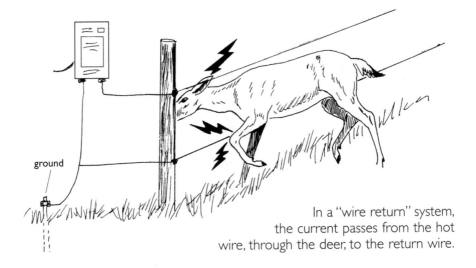

In a "wire return" system, the current passes from the hot wire, through the deer, to the return wire.

fencing supplies are available) to each at the desired height for each wire.

An effective generic earth-return fence design uses four evenly spaced strands of electrified wire, the lowest strung about a foot above the ground, the highest about four to five feet high. Personal experience in the Pacific Northwest has proved this design effective against deer in the region. It is interesting to note, however, that if the fence is turned off, the deer quickly realize it can't harm them and often walk right through the wires.

Aluminum wire, though highly conductive, may not be a good choice if your fence lies in an area where tree limbs could fall on it or livestock could run into it. It breaks too easily. A heavy-gauge, electric fence wire will save many headaches. Also, be careful not to install the wire within half an inch of any metal surface, including steel fence posts, gate hinges, or nails or fence staples in fence posts. The current can arc through the metal and ground out the system at that point. A tricky failure to find. Also, thoroughly flag the fence line; colored surveyor's tape, tied around the wire at intervals, works great. It's cheap and very visible. Not only will this tip off the deer that a new barrier is in place and speed their recognition of the boundaries, but it will also remind the neighbors where your fence is.

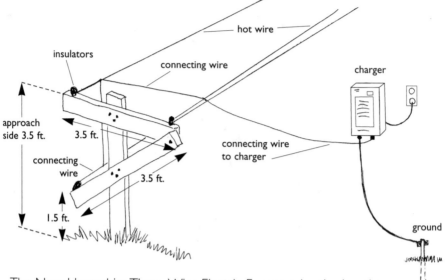

hot wire

insulators

connecting wire

charger

approach side 3.5 ft.

3.5 ft.

connecting wire to charger

connecting wire

3.5 ft.

1.5 ft.

ground

The New Hampshire Three-Wire Electric Fence varies the location of the shocking wires.

Electric fences require careful routine checks to be sure nothing has come into contact with the wire. Something as seemingly insignificant as a blade of tall grass can complete the circuit and ground out the system, rendering it useless. Be especially vigilant in checking your fence lines after storms, as grass or brush can blow onto the wires, causing a short. Always turn off the charger before attempting any repairs to the fence.

New Hampshire Three-Wire Electric Fence

The New Hampshire Three-Wire Electric Fence utilizes the high-and-wide approach. It is recommended for areas with low deer pressure. The angles of the design place the wires at different levels and widths. As illustrated, the fence is made from one-by-two-inch wood (scraps or new lumber), nails, insulators, wire (preferably eighteen-gauge copper-covered steel-core wire), a charger, ground wire, and grounding rods. This design is best in areas that receive little or no snow since it is close enough to the ground to be shorted out by heavy snowfall.

Another version of the same basic design uses alternating rows of fence posts but attaches the wire according to the same dimensions shown.

Penn State Five-Wire Outrigger Electric Fence

The Penn State Five-Wire Outrigger Electric Fence design is recommended for small-to-moderate acreage with moderate deer pressure. It calls for high-tensile New Zealand wire (12½ gauge, 200,000 psi) and special in-line wire tighteners that maintain the tension at 250 pounds. Special crimping sleeves are used wherever the wire is spliced to maintain the strength of the fence. Sturdy corner posts and supports are necessary to withstand the high tension, which ensures that the wire can absorb the force of deer running into it. Precise spacings of the wire prevent deer from going through the fence, while the height and width, as determined by electrified outriggers, ensure that deer won't go over. The lowest wire on the fence is set ten to twelve inches from the ground, which means all brush and grass must be cleared from the path of the fence and kept down. A high-voltage, low-impedance charger grounded with about twenty feet of rod or pipe gives the system its shocking power.

Variations of the fence have been used in different settings, with shorter versions serving well to protect small areas. If necessary, standard electric fence wire can be substituted for the New Zealand wire. The fence won't be as strong but will be less expensive to construct.

PROS AND CONS: The design is very well thought out and effective, but harder to put together than other types of electric fence. New Zealand wire and fence supplies are expensive but tough and long-lasting.

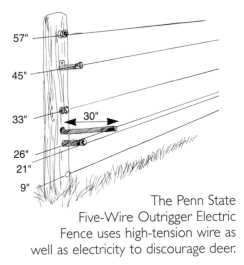

The Penn State Five-Wire Outrigger Electric Fence uses high-tension wire as well as electricity to discourage deer.

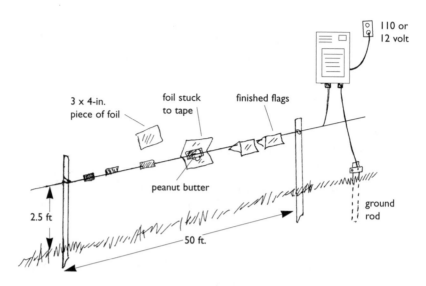

110 or 12 volt

3 x 4-in. piece of foil

foil stuck to tape

finished flags

peanut butter

ground rod

2.5 ft

50 ft.

The Minnesota DNR Fence baits the deer and then zaps them.

Minnesota DNR Electric Fence

A simple electric fence developed by the Minnesota Department of Natural Resources proves that we can so outwit deer. Folks that use it are delighted with the concept, and many have come up with embellishments. Basically, the idea is to lure the deer to the fence and then to teach them to avoid contact.

This design works best for areas of under twelve acres that suffer from only light deer pressure. If erected early, before deer pressure becomes more intense, it continues to protect your yard because the deer have *already* learned that it's off-limits.

Before setting up the fence, remove any grass or underbrush that could possibly come in contact with the wire. Set posts (wooden or steel) no more than fifty feet apart. The fence uses only a single electrified wire, which hangs about two and a half feet above the ground (if it sags, space the posts closer together). Attach insulators to the posts, string the wire through the insulators, and connect a grounding rod and fence charger.

Now for the secret weapon: The fence beckons unsuspecting deer to get zapped on the nose by baiting them with the irresistible aroma of peanut butter. One sniff and *"zzzaappp."* Off they go before they know what got them.

There are several ways to attach the peanut butter bait. The original idea was to wrap pieces of adhesive tape to the wire at three-foot intervals and attach pieces of heavy-duty aluminum foil (about four inches square) to the tape. The inside of the foil flags was then spread with a mixture of peanut oil and peanut butter to tantalize the deer. As more people have experimented with the design different approaches have sprung up, including the use of spring-loaded clips to attach the peanut butter flags. These are quicker to install and less likely to be blown against the post by the wind, which causes the fence to short out. However you attach the peanut butter bait, be sure to change it every three or four weeks, as it eventually becomes rancid.

GATES AND BYPASSES

Another way in which we sometimes unwittingly negate a good fence is with a bad gate. Gates must be as impenetrable as the fence or deer will quickly find the opening and invite themselves in.

Gates for wire or mesh fences can be constructed of the same wire or mesh strung across a frame built to the same height as the fence. Attach the gate on heavy-duty hinges to a solid, braced post. Wide gates, such as those for driveways or field equipment, may need to be supported from above to prevent sagging. A guy wire attached to a higher support post will help to disperse the pull of the gate on the support. Driveway gates can be constructed as double or single panels. Double panels must meet closely in the middle and be secured together to prevent deer from squeezing through.

Walk-throughs and stiles are options for deer-proof fences. Deer cannot maneuver the twists of the walk-through, nor are they apt to march over a stile. When a gate would leave a gap, consider one of these instead.

For a wide-mesh gate, a guy wire helps disperse the added weight.

Electric fence plans rarely include instructions for gates. Once the current is broken, no more electric fence, so gates must either be electrified or designed so that the current bypasses the gateway. One way to bypass the gate is to run the fence wire high above it; another is to bury the wire within an insulated sleeve (old rubber hose works fine) and reattach it to the fence on the opposite side.

Electric gate handles resemble oversized insulators with a hook at one end and an attachment for the fence wire at the other. The handles are spring loaded to keep the fence tension constant and to allow you to open the "gate" easily by pulling the handle up and unhooking it from the fence wire on the opposite side of the gate. Rig the handles so that when you unhook them the electric current disengages in the handle, the gate wire, and any part of the fence downcurrent from the gate. You can set the handle down without having a live wire on the ground.

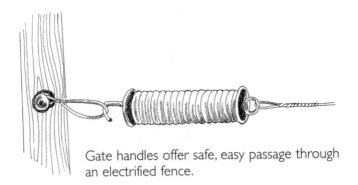

Gate handles offer safe, easy passage through an electrified fence.

PROTECTING INDIVIDUAL PLANTS

Fencing in vulnerable or especially valuable plants does not necessarily require fencing the entire estate. As an alternative, protect individual plants with little fences of their own. You can easily fashion wire or mesh cages to protect any size plants — from a row of newly emerging lettuce to the trunks of young fruit trees. Drape plastic netting over susceptible plants or entire beds or borders. Drive stakes on either side of shrubs and wrap chicken wire around and over them. For portable protection that can be used over and over on different plants, build a framework of scrap lumber or PVC pipe and attach mesh to form a protective cage. Heavier-duty wire mesh, such as hardware cloth (small-mesh wire), can be bent into shape and positioned to protect plants without additional support. Be sure to anchor cages in place so that deer can't nudge them over.

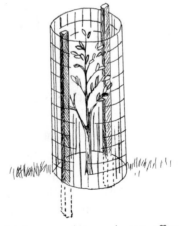

Plants may not need protection indefinitely. For instance, once fruit has been harvested or small trees have matured, they need not remain

Nylon or wire mesh can effectively protect vulnerable plants.

Protective trunk wrap can prevent damage caused by bucks rubbing their antlers.

covered. Unlike an entire perimeter fence, individual plant protectors are easy to remove.

Protect the trunks of trees and shrubs from rubbing damage caused by amorous bucks by wrapping them with a protective trunk wrap. Garden centers carry products made especially for this purpose, such as Vexar tubes, or substitute strips cut from old inner tubes.

CANINE INSURANCE

Even in areas experiencing high deer pressure, installing a strong deer-proof fence will probably offer your yard or garden adequate protection. But if you want additional insurance, or if you'd prefer a less elaborate security arrangement, add a dog.

Deer avoid dogs. And for good reason. Dogs have replaced wolves, cougars, and bears as the number one nonhuman predator of deer. Especially in deep or crusted snow, where deer cannot outrun them, dogs take a serious toll. They still have that predator instinct and the deer know it.

Not that having a guard dog for your garden doesn't carry its own costs and responsibilities. To begin with, very few areas

The No-Fence Dog Fence

Hate the chain, but not crazy about fencing in your yard? Another great technological advance for gardeners is the no-fence dog fence, sold under such brand names as Invisible Fence and DogWatch. A thin cable is buried around the perimeter of the area to which your dog will have access. The dog wears a radio collar that transmits a signal to warn him whenever he ventures near the line. If he gets too close, *zzzaapp!*

After a brief training period most dogs learn the limits and stay within their "territory," although some will ignore the shocks if the incentive — giving chase to a rabbit or, unfortunately, a deer — is strong enough. The breeding and individual personality of your dog are probably the deciding factors. If an electronic fence succeeds in restraining your dog, you can be sure that deer (and other sneak thieves) will give the loose canine, and your garden, a wide berth.

Two words of caution about these electronic fences: First, don't waste your money on cheap imitations, which can put your dog at risk; and second, before letting your dog outside, know what else lurks in your neighborhood. Just because your dog can't get out, doesn't mean other animals can't get in.

allow free-roaming dogs anymore. Loose dogs often band together, or "pack." When they do, it's as if ancient memories of their wolf past suddenly revive, and family pets revert to wild-eyed, *dangerous* beasts. Dogs in packs attack livestock, other pets, wildlife, and people. Things your gentle pet would never do, its alter-in-pack-ego does with impunity. Many areas allow people to shoot dogs on sight that are menacing or chasing livestock or deer. Therefore, for its own safety, that of the neighborhood, and your own peace of mind, the first consideration of dog ownership is keeping the dog under control. For that, you have two basic options: chaining or fencing.

Chaining vs. Fencing

Life at the end of a chain is a miserable existence. And as far as protecting the garden goes, the deer will quickly realize that the dog can go only so far and will learn to ignore him. After a while the dog will realize that the deer are ignoring him and are no longer fun to bark at. Stories abound of dogs sleeping while deer browse nearby. One solution is to move the chain from place to place every few days, which does help to keep the deer confused.

Before deciding to chain your dog, also consider this: If deer have found their way to your yard, what else has? Other wildlife, such as coyotes, have become just as adapted to the presence of humans, and a dog at the end of a chain is at their mercy. In some areas larger predators, such as cougars and bears, have followed their prey, the deer, and a chained dog has no hope against such an adversary. Other dogs allowed to run loose have ganged up against their chained counterparts, with sickening results. So don't chain your dog.

Instead, fence. The wonderful thing about fencing a garden or yard with a dog inside is that you needn't worry so much about fencing the *deer out* as fencing the *dog in*. Which is a darned sight easier to do.

The height and sturdiness of a dog-proof fence depends on the height and sturdiness of the dog. Medium-sized dogs can jump over a three-foot-tall fence, but generally don't attempt it if they don't have to. A four-foot fence of wire mesh, plastic mesh, or wood, supplemented with a strand or two of electrified wire, will keep in almost any dog. Choose from a standard chain-link fence, a charming white-painted picket fence, or any style that suits your fancy. A dog fence is ideal for many people because it allows the dog free run of the yard and garden, which means he gets lots of attention from his people and can serve as an alarm system for everything from deer to burglars. As part of a security system for your home, the fence may even add value to your property.

Choosing a Dog

Do you need to invest in a purebred, guard-trained Doberman? Of course not. Any dog that looks like a dog, smells like a dog, and barks and runs around like a dog is dog enough to make deer nervous. Again, those ancient wolf-pack memories may be to blame. Perhaps the deer see, smell, and hear *dog*, but register *wolf*.

In general, dogs bred for guarding, hunting, or herding make the best "deer dogs." Such guardians as Dobermans (my favorite), Great Danes, German shepherds, komondors, and Great Pyrenees top the list. Hunting breeds, especially hounds, will sound the alarm when deer come around, but trained hunting dogs are taught to ignore deer scent as "trash" because it distracts them. Herding dogs, such as Border collies, collies, and the many types of shepherds, have the instinct to chase and may or may not be inclined to bark at the intruders.

Before investing in a purebred, you may want to take a trip to the pound. First and foremost, look for the same things you would look for in any pet dog. A dog that seems happy to see you is a good start. But if he's bounding around uncontrollably in the kennel, he's apt to behave the same way in your garden. Pick a dog you want to live with. Second, look for a dog that exhibits some of the breeding mentioned above. Most animal shelters will try to venture a guess at the breed (or breeds). Third, look for a bright-eyed, alert dog of medium to large size that will look you in the eye and respond to changing tones of voice.

Community Efforts 7

When it comes to deer, the comfort zone for some gardeners might as well be the twilight zone. The issues and degrees of concern vary so widely that gardeners in different parts of the country may sound as though they aren't even talking about the same subject when they discuss deer damage. For those under truly heavy deer pressure, the problem and their reactions to it are more severe than for those whose gardens haven't been ransacked beyond recognition. For many, the deer issue goes far beyond an individual problem — it has become a community concern.

MANAGEMENT STRATEGIES

The issue of deer management is most charged in areas where the deer population (usually white-tailed deer) exceeds the ability of the natural habitat to sustain it. Intense deer pressure on yards, gardens, orchards, crops, and nurseries becomes a major economic concern as well as an emotional issue. Studies in various states routinely put the estimated crop damage in the tens of millions of dollars — and that doesn't reflect the damage to private yards and gardens. Compound deer overpopulation with a bad winter or decimated forage (which is the predictable result of deer overpopulation), and the results can be gruesome.

Even in areas where no one questions that the deer population exceeds reasonable limits, competing interests often offer very different ideas about how to lower it. The three most commonly discussed alternatives call for letting nature take its course, hunting, and birth control.

Nature's Course

The "let-them-be" approach drops the problem back in Mother Nature's lap. Trouble is, Mother Nature didn't cause

Deer Counts Count

Wildlife agencies consider accurate counts of deer critical to management strategies, yet not everyone agrees on the methods of counting or the actual count. Counts may be taken in several ways, including deer drives, in which deer are herded past posted counters who tally them up, and aerial surveys, which tend to be less accurate.

If the accuracy of the count is questioned, it places in doubt the number of deer that need to be removed. For example, if a certain area can optimally sustain 25 deer per square mile, and the count declares there to be 240 deer in a four-square-mile area, then how many deer should face removal? What if the count was too low? Removing too few deer is a wasted effort: The slight temporary dip in population can trigger more energetic repopulation. What if the count was too high? If only about 150 deer actually live in the area, then removing 140 of them in an effort to reach that optimal ratio would instead wipe out the population.

this mess and isn't all that well equipped to handle such extremes in a kind manner. Under normal conditions deer populations do not exceed the capacity of the habitat because each spring, before new fawns are born, the does drive last year's babies out into the world. This dispersal is one of nature's many ways of keeping the population balanced to the land. But deer "left to nature" in severely overpopulated areas have nowhere to go. Surrounding areas are already packed with other deer. Whitetails, especially, will occupy their ancestral grounds for generations, regardless of its condition.

Deer left to nature in such circumstances lead pitiful lives and meet tragic deaths. They gradually weaken, sometimes over generations, until food totally disappears, and then they linger on until death overtakes them. Weakened deer are sickly, often riddled inside and out by parasites, easily devastated by disease, and often in pain from their infirmities. In winter they die by the hordes, breaking their necks on fences that healthy deer haughtily bound over, and falling victim to predators or dogs, sometimes being eaten alive, too weak to resist. Or they simply lie down and do not get up. To suggest that nature will solve this problem is irresponsible, cruel, and ignorant.

Hunting

To some, hunting is merely a sport, or perhaps a way to put meat on the table. Others consider it a practical management tool. And still others regard legalized deer hunting as unconscionable slaughter. However you look at it, the fact remains that deer hunting has always been a part of the American culture and has evolved into an $11 billion-a-year industry.

In 1995 hunters killed approximately six million whitetailed deer, which hardly dented a population estimated at over twenty-five million. Biologists explain that to *stabilize* a deer population, each year 40 percent of the females must die, naturally or otherwise. Obviously, to *reduce* any given population requires that even more deer be taken from the overall population.

Many areas have tried to stabilize the deer population by regulated hunts — in extreme cases employing more creative approaches, such as Wisconsin's "Earn a Buck" program, in which hunters earn the right to go after a set of antlers by first bringing down a doe. In isolated areas where deer densities have reached intolerable levels, controlled hunts often permit expert hunters to take specified numbers of deer as part of the community effort to reduce the populations as quickly and humanely as possible. In effect, human hunters replace displaced natural predators.

So why doesn't hunting work better as a population management tool? Several reasons. The country's twelve million to fifteen million deer hunters, of whom half or fewer kill a deer each year, harvest too high a proportion of bucks — the healthiest ones, with the most impressive antlers, rather than the weak or inferior. They also take their prey all at once in any given area, thus creating a short-term dip in the population, which deer instinctively fill. Fewer deer equals less competition equals higher reproduction. This supports the contention of many antihunting groups that hunting management schemes, inadvertently or otherwise, *create* overpopulation, thereby maintaining the apparent necessity for hunting. If human hunters behaved more like their wild counterparts, killing the lesser animals and leaving the fittest to survive, over an extended period of time rather than just prior to or in the midst of the annual mating season, they might be more successful at affecting the overall numbers.

Another drawback to relying on the human predator for population control is that he can't work in his own backyard. Many of the heaviest concentrations of deer occur in and around suburban housing developments, golf courses, parks, and even college campuses. Hunting in such areas just isn't practical or safe. Furthermore, in many deer-dense areas the deer are virtually tame, and public sentiment tends to run deeply against shooting them.

Immunocontraception

The newest approach to deer overpopulation involves slowing down the rate of reproduction. Nature does so when circumstances are particularly tough. Starvation and harsh winters often result in fewer fawns being born. Does may bear only one fawn instead of the usual twins, produce a stillborn, or in extreme circumstances abort or resorb fetuses. Wildlife biologists seek a way to spare the deer the stress of the natural method while achieving the same outcome, fewer fawns.

Birth control for wildlife began in the early 1970s in an effort to control the numbers of feral horses. Field testing eventually resulted in success rates of over 90 percent. In 1987 testing began in isolated deer populations. Dr. Jay Kirkpatrick, the leader in the field, expects a 95 percent success rate.

Immunocontraceptive vaccines are administered by dart, which minimizes stress to the animal and reduces the time, trouble, and expense of dosing. To date, a two-dose program has been most effective, but efforts to develop a reliable one-dose vaccine are continuing. The PZP vaccine used in deer incorporates a protein from pigs that normally causes the sperm to attach to the egg. When injected into a doe, this protein produces antibodies that attack the doe's own sperm-attachment proteins. Though the doe mates normally, a buck's sperm cannot bind to the egg and conception does not occur. In addition to carrying no health risk for the deer, the proteins in the vaccine pose no threat to people, including those who eat venison from treated does.

Contained populations offer the best opportunity to administer immunocontraception and to monitor the effects. Studies at Fire Island National Seashore in New York and the Smithsonian Conservation and Research Center at Front Royal, Virginia, have produced success rates of between 70 and 100 percent in terms of prevented pregnancies. In large, free-roaming populations of deer, however, use of the vaccine may not be practical. Wildlife managers disagree, and testing continues.

FUTURE PROSPECTS

Many areas — particularly northern New Jersey, parts of New York, much of New England, Missouri, Wisconsin, and California — suffer from severe deer pressure. In affected regions the issue of deer control continues to be hotly debated, not only because of the damage deer inflict, but also because the deer are suffering — unthrifty in appearance, unhealthy, and starving. Indeed, in some areas the quality of the entire deer population is deteriorating. Average size is declining and bucks are producing smaller antlers. As Aldo Leopold commented half a century ago, "There are no stags in the woods today like those whose antlers decorated the walls of feudal castles."

> "Soil, water, vegetation and wildlife cannot be managed separately for they are not separate entities but integral parts of the whole."
> Leonard Lee Rue III, *The Deer of North America*, 1989

What has yet to be tried? Perhaps dominant bucks that have been rendered infertile could be introduced into areas of overpopulation. Where deer herds have deteriorated genetically due to inbreeding or environmental conditions, superior bucks could be relocated to strengthen faltering gene pools. Outlying areas, away from residential districts, could be opened up to deer dispersal by regulated burns.

Obviously, managing deer presents daunting challenges, not the least of which is balancing competing public interests and sentiments. The focus must be on the long-term welfare of the deer and of the communities in which they live. Healthy deer, in manageable numbers, can be a blessing and a benefit to all. And with population crises managed and adequate wild food available, we could concentrate on keeping a reasonable number of deer away from our landscape and garden plants.

APPENDIX

DETERRENT SOURCES

Predator Scents

Bobcat, coyote, and fox urine
J&C Marketing, Inc.
P.O. Box 125
Hampden, ME 04444
800-218-1749

Coyote urine
Deerbusters
800-248-DEER (3337)
Fax: 301-694-9254
Web Site: http://www.deerbusters.com

Scent and Taste Deterrents

Deer Off
58 High Valley Way
Stamford, CT 06903-2714
203-968-8485
800-DEER-OFF (333-7633)
Fax: 203-968-2882
Not approved for use on food crops.

Deer-Away/Big Game Repellent
800-642-2112
One application works reliably for a
month. Available in five-gallon liquid
or twenty-pound powder. One gallon or
one pound treats sixty feet of shrubs.
Approved for evergreens, fruit, citrus,
and ornamental trees and shrubs.

Deer-Outahere
Black Hills Energy Inc.
4447 South Canyon Road, Suite 1
Rapid City, SD 57702
A money-back-guaranteed, chemical-free
homemade deer repellent recipe.

Hinder
Deerbusters
See under "Predator Scents".

Hot Sauce Animal Repellent
Deerbusters
See under "Predator Scents".
The active ingredient is capsaicin. Repels
deer, rabbits, and mice. Best applied
before fruit set or after harvest. Approved
for ornamentals, fruit, nut trees, vegetables, shrubs, and vines. Most effective
when used with an antidesiccant sticking
agent, such as Vapor Gard.

Milorganite
Milorganite Division — MM SD
1101 N. Market Street
Milwaukee, WI 53202
414-225-3333
800-287-9645

N.I.M.B.Y.
6540 Martin Luther King Drive
St. Louis, MO 63133
314-385-0076
Fax: 314-385-0062
E-mail: dmxinds@aol.com
Web Site: http://www.nimby.com
An all-natural squirrel and deer
repellent. Approval pending for use on
food crops.

No-Bite Tablets
Deerbusters
See under "Predator Scents".

Repellent Accessories

Garden Scent-ry
Gardener's Supply Co.
800-863-1700
Fax: 800-551-6712
Web Site: http://www.gardeners.com
Covered reservoir that protects any
repellent, from hair to wildcat urine,
from the elements. Made from recycled
plastic, it can be staked to the ground or
hung from a limb.

Deer Fencing

Black Plastic Mesh Fencing
Benner's Gardens
6974 Upper York Road
New Hope, PA 18938
800-753-4660
Fax: 215-477-9429
Lightweight, virtually invisible, durable
black plastic deer netting available in
330-foot rolls in heights of 4, 5, 6, and
7.5 feet. Stakes also available for pinning
the fence to the ground. Also, lightweight black plastic bird netting
(0.25-inch mesh) available in 125-foot-
rolls, 7 and 14 feet high.

Gardener's Supply Company
See under "Repellent Accessories".

Scaring Devices

*Propane Cannons, Sonic Bombs,
Ultrasonic Warning Devices, Solar
Floodlights, Wireless Deer Alert
Security System (Motion detector)*
Deerbusters
See under "Predator Scents".

INFORMATION SOURCES

Advocacy Groups

Whitetails Unlimited
P.O. Box 760
Sturgeon Bay, WI 54235-0720
414-743-6777
Pro-hunting deer group

**The Humane Society
of the United States**
2100 L Street, NW
Washington, DC 20037
202-452-1100
Web Site: http://www.hsus.org
Antihunting group

State Wildlife Agencies

Alabama Game and Fish
64 N. Union Street
Montgomery, AL 36130
334-242-3465
Web Site: http://www.wrldnet.net/

Alaska Department of Fish and Game
P.O. Box 25526
Juneau, AK 99802
907-465-4190 or 907-465-2376
Web Site: http://www.state.ak.us/
    local/akpages/FISH.GAME/wildlife/
    wildmain.htm

Arizona Game and Fish Department
2221 W. Greenway Road
Phoenix, AZ 85023
Web Site: http://www.gf.state.a2.us/
welcome.html

Arkansas Game and Fish Department
No. 2 Natural Resources DL
Little Rock, AR 72205
501-223-6300
Web Site: http://www.outdoors.net/
arkansas

California Department of Fish and Game
1416 Ninth Street
Sacramento, CA 95814
916-653-7664
Web Site: http://www.dfg.ca.gov

Colorado Division of Wildlife
6060 Broadway
Denver, CO 80216
303-297-1192
Web Site: www.dnr.state.co.us/wildlife

Connecticut Department of the Environment
165 Capitol Avenue
Hartford, CT 06106
860-424-3011
Web Site: http://www.connecticut.com/

Delaware Department of Natural Resources
P.O. Box 1401
89 Kings Highway
Dover, DE 19903
302-739-5297
Web Site: http://www.

Florida Game and Fresh Water Fish
620 S. Meridian Street
Tallahassee, FL 32399
904-488-4676
Web Site: http://www.state.fl.us/gfc

Georgia Department of Natural Resources
2189 Northlake Parkway
Building 10, Suite 108
Tucker, GA 30084
770-414-3333
Web Site: http://www.dnr.state.ga.us/
index.htm

Idaho Department of Fish and Game
600 South Walnut Street
P.O. Box 25
Boise, ID 83707
208-334-3700
Web Site: www.id.us/fishgame

Illinois Department of Conservation
Lincoln Tower Plaza
524 S. Second Street
Springfield, IL 62701
217-782-6384
Web Site: http://www.dnr.state.il.us/

Indiana Department of Natural Resources
402 W. Washington
Indianapolis, IN 46204
317-232-4080
Web Site: www.dnr.state.in.us/fishwild

Iowa Department of Natural Resources (NBEF)
Wallace State Office Building
Des Moines, IA 50319
515-281-5918
Web Site: www.state.ia.us/government/
dnr

Kansas Department of Wildlife and Parks
Route 2, Box 54A
Pratt, KS 67124
316-672-5911
Web Site: http://www.lnk.org/public/
kbwp

Kentucky Department of Fish and Wildlife Resources
1 Game Farm Road
Frankfort, KY 40601
502-564-4336
Web Site: www.state.ky.us/agencies/
fw/kdfwr.htm

Louisiana Department of Wildlife
P.O. Box 98000
Baton Rouge, LA 70898
504-765-2925
Web Site: www.wlf.state.la.us

Maine Department of Inland Fisheries and Wildlife
284 State Street Station 41
Augusta, ME 04333
207-287-8000
Web Site: www.state.me.us/ifw/
homepage.htm

Maryland Department of Natural Resources
Tawes State Office Building
Annapolis, MD 21401
410-260-8540

Massachusetts Division of Fisheries and Wildlife
100 Cambridge Street
Boston, MA 02202
617-727-3151
Web Site: www.magnet.state.ma.us/
dfwele/dfw/dfwcallw.htm

Michigan Department of Natural Resources
Box 30028
Lansing, MI 489091
517-3731-1263
Web Site: http://www.dnr.state.mi.us/

Minnesota Department of Natural Resources
DNR Building
500 Lafayette
St. Paul, MN 55155-4026
612-296-6157
Web Site: http://www.dnr.state.ms.us/

Mississippi Department of Wildlife Conservation
P.O. Box 451
Jackson, MS 39205-0451
601-362-9212

Missouri Department of Conservation
P.O. Box 180
Jefferson City, MO 65102-0180
573-751-4115

Montana Department of Fish, Wildlife, and Parks
1420 E. Sixth Avenue
Helena, MT 59620
406-444-2535 or 406-444-5354
Web Site: http://nris.mt.gov

Nebraska Game and Parks Commission
2200 N. 33rd Street
P.O. Box 30370
Lincoln, NE 68503
402-471-0641
Web Site: http://www.ngpc.state.ne.us/
gp.html

Nevada Department of Conservation and Natural Resources Division of Wildlife
1100 Valley Road
Carson City, NV 89701
702-688-1500
Web Site: http://vegasonline.com

New Hampshire Fish and Game
2 Hazen Drive
Concord, NH 03301
603-271-3421
Web Site: http://www.wildlife.state.nh.us/
home.html

New Jersey Department of the
Environment
CN-400
Trenton, NJ 08625
609-292-2965
Web Site: www.state.nj.us/dep/fgw

New Mexico Department of Game
and Fish
P.O. Box 25112
Santa Fe, NM 87504
505-827-7911
Web Site: http://gmfsh.state.nm.us/

New York Department of
Environment
50 Wolf Road
Albany, NY 12233-4750
518-457-5690

North Carolina Wildlife Commission
512 N. Salisbury
Raleigh, NC 27611
919-733-3391 or 888-248-6834
Web Site: http://www.ehnr.state.nc.us/
EHNR

North Dakota Game and Fish
100 N. Bismarck Expressway
Bismarck, ND 58501
701-328-6300
Web Site: http://www.state.nd.us/gnf/

Ohio Department of Natural
Resources
1840 Belcher Drive
Columbus, OH 43224
614-265-6300
Web Site: http://www.dnr.ohio.gov/odnr/
wildlife/wildlife.html

Oklahoma Conservation Commission
1801 N. Lincoln, P.O. Box 53465
Oklahoma City, OK 73105
405-521-3851
Web Site: http://www.state.ok.us/

Oregon Department of Fish
and Wildlife
P.O. Box 59
Portland, OR 97207
503-872-5775
Web Site: http://www.orst.edu/dept/
fishwild

Pennsylvania Department of
Conservation
2001 Elmerton Avenue
Harrisburg, PA 17110
717-787-6286
Web Site: http://www.dcnrstate.pa.us/

Rhode Island Department of the
Environment
235 Promenade Street
Providence, RI 02908
401-789-3094
Web Site: http://www

South Carolina Wildlife and Marine
P.O. Box 11710
Columbia, SC 29211
803-734-3843
Web Site: http://www.dnr.state.sc.us

South Dakota Department of Game,
Fish, and Parks
412 West Anderson
Pierre, SD 57501
605-773-3485
Web Site: http://www.state.sd.us/state/
executive/gfp/gfp.html

Tennessee Wildlife Resources
P.O. Box 40747
Nashville, TN 37204
615-781-6622
Web Site: http://www.state.tn.us/twra/
index.html

Texas Parks and Wildlife
4200 Smith School Road
Austin, TX 78744
512-389-4800 or 800-792-1112
Web Site: http://www.tpwd.state.tx.us/
  hunt/pubhunt/php.htm

Utah Division of Wildlife Resources
1596 W. North Temple
Salt Lake City, UT 85116
801-538-4700
Web Site: http://www.nr.state.ut.us/

Vermont Fish and Wildlife
103 S. Main Street 10 South
Waterbury, VT 05761-0501
802-479-3242
Web Site: http://www.pbpub.com/
  hunting/hunt.htm

Virginia Department of Game and Inland Fisheries
4010 W. Broad Street
Box 11104
Richmond, VA 23230
804-367-1000
Web Site: http://www.state.va.us/

Washington Department of Wildlife
600 Capitol Way N
Olympia, WA 98501-1091
360-902-2200
Web Site: http://www.wa.gov/wdfw/

West Virginia Wildlife Resources Department
State Capitol Complex — Building 3
Charleston, WV 25305
304-558-2771
Web Site: http://www.abi.org/nhp/us/wv/

Wisconsin Department of Natural Resources
P.O. Box 7921
Madison, WI 53707
608-266-1877

Wyoming Department of Game and Fish
5400 Bishop Boulevard
Cheyenne, WY 82006
307-777-4601
Web Site: http://gf.state.wy.us/

Internet Sites

http://www.deer.com
Web site for *Deer and Deer Hunting* magazine, with loads of links.

http://deerbusters.com
Deerbusters' products for deer control, links.

http://www.cdc.gov/ncidod/diseases/ lyme/lymedis.htm
Centers for Disease Control (CDC) site for information on Lyme disease.

http://www.ndsu.nodak.edu/instruct/ devold/twrid/html/sites.htm
Wildlife web site directory information on everything from animal behavior to zoonoses (animal-to-human communicable diseases).

http://www.uri.edu/artsci/zool/ ticklab
Resource for tick-related information.

http://trine.com/GardenNet
All-purpose gardeners' forum.

http://www.garden.com/cgi-bin/ rell.o/gedesign
Garden design. Fill out the on-line form with your garden's conditions, click on the box that says "deer resistant," and a plant list is instantly generated. Neat!

INDEX

Hearing, sense of, 15, 106–11
Hedges, **64**
Herbs, 92
Hot pepper spray, 99–101
Humans
    accidents/injuries involving deer, 43–46
    deer becoming accustomed to, 28–29, 86–87
    hair, as deer deterrent, 91
    health concerns, deer and, 46–48
Hunting. *See* Shooting/hunting deer

I

Immunocontraception, 144
Injuries, deer-related, 43–46
Internet sites, 151

L

Lawn ornaments, 72
Lyme disease, 46–48

M

Mechanical gizmos, 104–5
Minnesota DNR Electric Fence, *132*, 132–33
Monofilament line, as deer deterrent, 111–12
Moose, 22, **23**
Mothballs, as deer repellent, 94
Motion detectors, 106, 147
Mule deer, 21, **23**

N

Naphthalene, 94
Netting, prefab deer, *125*, 125–26
New Hampshire Three-Wire Electric Fence, *130*, 130–31
Noise repellents, 106–11
Nonelectric fences, 121–26

O

Opaque deer fence, 125
Ornamental grasses, **59**. *See also* Plants

P

Penn State Five-Wire Outrigger Electric Fence, 131, *131*
Pepper spray, as deer deterrent, 99–101
Perennials, **56**. *See also* Plants
Plants. *See also* Deer deterrents; Deer-o-scaping; Gardens
    damaged, 42–43
    deer avoid eating, 54–55, **56–67**
    deer prefer eating, 52–54, **53**
    protecting individual, 135–36
    systemic aversives, 103
    testing for palatability, 68–69
    that repel deer, **68**, 92, 103
Poisoning deer, 114, 116
Predators
    attracting unwanted, 97, 115
    deer avoiding, 15–17, 86
    tankage and, 115
    urine/feces, as deer repellents, 97–98, 146
Prefab deer netting, *125*, 125–26
Processed sewage, as deer repellent, 95–96

R

Radios, as deer repellents, 108–9
Repellents. *See* Deer deterrents
Roses, **66–67**
Rotten eggs, as deer repellent, 92–93
Rural areas, 50
Rutting behavior. *See* Bucks

S

Safety. *See* Health and safety issues
Scaring devices, as deer deterrents, 103–6, 147
Scat, 41
Scent repellents, 88–98, 146
Seasons, behavioral adjustments and, 29–36
Senses, deer's physical, 15–16, 25, 88
Sewage, processed, as deer repellent, 95–96

Shade. *See* Boggy, shady gardens; Dry, shady gardens
Shooting/hunting deer, 114, 116, 142–43
Shrubs. *See* Trees/shrubs
Sight, sense of, 15–16, 103–6
Slanted deer fence, 122–23, *123*
Smell, sense of, 15, 25, 88–98
Soap, as deer deterrent, 90–91, 101–2
Sonic warning devices, 110
Speed, to avoid predators, 16
Spray deterrents
　hot pepper, 99–101
　soap, 101–2
Spring. *See* Seasons
Sprinklers, as deer deterrents, 114
Standard deer fence, *121*, 121–22
Starvation, 26, 36, 54, 99, 142
State wildlife agencies, 147–51
Suburban areas
　deer behavior in, 28–29
　deer damage, limiting, 51
　deer deterrents in, 86
　as deer habitat, 10–13
　garden damage, 37–43
Summer. *See* Seasons
Sunny gardens with ample moisture, 73, 76, 77
Swimming pools, 45, 46
Systemic aversives, 103

T
Tails, deer identification and, 18
Tankage, 97, 115
Taste repellents, 98–103, 146
Teeth marks, on damaged plants, 42–43
Territorial limits, 27–28
Thiram, as deer deterrent, 102–3
Tick-borne diseases, 46–48
Timed sprinklers, as deer deterrents, 114
Touch, surprise physical, as deer deterrents, 111–14
Tracks, identifying, 40

Traffic collisions, with deer, 43–44, 110–11
Trapping deer, as deterrent, 116
Trees/shrubs, 38, **53, 59–64,** 136. *See also* Deer damage; Deer-o-scaping

U
Ultrasonic devices, as deer deterrents, 111
Upright fence, converting, *124,* 124–25
Urban areas, 51–52
Urine or feces
　human, as deer deterrent, 115
　predator, as deer repellent, 97–98, 146

V
Vegetables, fruits and nuts, **65**
Vines, **53, 64.** *See also* Plants

W
Water supply, garden design and, 77, 79, 81
Whistles, 44, 110–11
White flags, as deer deterrents, 105–6
White-tailed deer, 20–21, **23**
Wildlife management, 114, 141, 147–51
Windows/glass, deer collisions with, 46
Winter. *See* Seasons
"Wire-return" electric fence system, 128, *129*

X
Xeriscaping, 49, 71–72

OTHER STOREY TITLES
YOU WILL ENJOY

Bugs, Slugs & Other Thugs, by Rhonda Massingham Hart. Includes hundreds of ways to stop pests without risk to the user or the environment, from folk remedies to the latest scientific discoveries. 224 pages. Paperback. ISBN 0-88266-664-9.

The Gardener's Weed Book: Earth-Safe Controls, by Barbara Pleasant. This comprehensive guide for beginners and experts explains how to understand, identify, and control weeds using earth-safe methods. 144 pages. Paperback. ISBN 0-88266-921-4.

The Gardener's Bug Book: Earth-Safe Insect Control, by Barbara Pleasant. This completely revised and updated garden guide shows how to identify and control more than 70 common garden insects using the best homemade and commercial control strategies. 160 pages. Paperback. ISBN 0-88266-609-6.

The Gardener's Guide to Plant Diseases: Earth-Safe Remedies, by Barbara Pleasant. The antidote to the 50 most common plant diseases, what they look like, where they're found, what to do about them, and what will happen to the plant. 192 pages. Paperback. ISBN 0-88266-274-0.

Fences for Pasture & Garden by Gail Damerow. The complete guide to choosing, planning, and building today's best fences: wire, rail, electric, high-tension, temporary, woven, and snow. Includes chapters on gates and trellises. 160 pages. Paperback. ISBN 0-88266-753-X.

These books and other Storey books are available at your bookstore, farm store, garden center, or directly from Storey Publishing, Schoolhouse Road, Pownal, Vermont 05261, or by calling 800-441-5700. www.storey.com